HBR'S 10 MUST READS

On
Creativity

HBR's 10 Must Reads series is the definitive collection of ideas and best practices for aspiring and experienced leaders alike. These books offer essential reading selected from the pages of *Harvard Business Review* on topics critical to the success of every manager.

Titles include:

HBR's 10 Must Reads 2015
HBR's 10 Must Reads 2016
HBR's 10 Must Reads 2017
HBR's 10 Must Reads 2018
HBR's 10 Must Reads 2019
HBR's 10 Must Reads 2020
HBR's 10 Must Reads 2021
HBR's 10 Must Reads for CEOs
HBR's 10 Must Reads for New Managers
HBR's 10 Must Reads on AI, Analytics, and the New Machine Age
HBR's 10 Must Reads on Boards
HBR's 10 Must Reads on Building a Great Culture
HBR's 10 Must Reads on Business Model Innovation
HBR's 10 Must Reads on Change Management
HBR's 10 Must Reads on Collaboration
HBR's 10 Must Reads on Communication
HBR's 10 Must Reads on Design Thinking
HBR's 10 Must Reads on Diversity
HBR's 10 Must Reads on Emotional Intelligence
HBR's 10 Must Reads on Entrepreneurship and Startups
HBR's 10 Must Reads on Innovation
HBR's 10 Must Reads on Leadership
HBR's 10 Must Reads on Leadership (Vol. 2)
HBR's 10 Must Reads on Leadership for Healthcare
HBR's 10 Must Reads on Leadership Lessons from Sports
HBR's 10 Must Reads on Making Smart Decisions
HBR's 10 Must Reads on Managing Across Cultures

HBR's 10 Must Reads on Managing in a Downturn
HBR's 10 Must Reads on Managing People
HBR's 10 Must Reads on Managing People (Vol. 2)
HBR's 10 Must Reads on Managing Risk
HBR's 10 Must Reads on Managing Yourself
HBR's 10 Must Reads on Mental Toughness
HBR's 10 Must Reads on Negotiation
HBR's 10 Must Reads on Nonprofits and the Social Sectors
HBR's 10 Must Reads on Public Speaking and Presenting
HBR's 10 Must Reads on Reinventing HR
HBR's 10 Must Reads on Sales
HBR's 10 Must Reads on Strategic Marketing
HBR's 10 Must Reads on Strategy
HBR's 10 Must Reads on Strategy (Vol. 2)
HBR's 10 Must Reads on Strategy for Healthcare
HBR's 10 Must Reads on Teams
HBR's 10 Must Reads on Women and Leadership
HBR's 10 Must Reads: The Essentials

HBR'S 10 MUST READS

On
Creativity

HARVARD BUSINESS REVIEW PRESS
Boston, Massachusetts

Library of Congress Cataloging-in-Publication Data

Title: HBR's 10 must reads on creativity.
Other titles: Harvard Business Review's ten must reads on creativity | HBR's 10 must reads (Series)
Description: Boston, Massachusetts : Harvard Business Review Press, [2020] | Series: HBR's 10 must reads | Includes index. |
Identifiers:L CCN 2020026437 (print) | LCCN 2020026438 (ebook) | ISBN 9781633699953 (paperback) | ISBN 9781633699960 (ebook other)
Subjects: LCSH: Creative ability in business. | Success in business.
Classifi cation: LCC HD53 .H393 2020 (print) | LCC HD53 (ebook) | DDC 658.4/094--dc23
LC record available at https://lccn.loc.gov/2020026437
LC ebook record available at https://lccn.loc.gov/2020026438

ISBN: 978-1-63369-997-7
eISBN:978- 1-63369-996-0

Contents

Reclaim Your Creative Confidence   1
by Tom Kelley and David Kelley

How to Kill Creativity   11
by Teresa M. Amabile

How Pixar Fosters Collective Creativity   33
by Ed Catmull

Putting Your Company's Whole Brain to Work   51
by Dorothy Leonard and Susaan Straus

Find Innovation Where You Least Expect It   69
by Tony McCaffrey and Jim Pearson

The Business Case for Curiosity   83
by Francesca Gino

Bring Your Breakthrough Ideas to Life   99
by Cyril Bouquet, Jean-Louis Barsoux, and Michael Wade

Collaborating with Creative Peers   119
by Kimberly D. Elsbach, Brooke Brown-Saracino, and Francis J. Flynn

Creativity Under the Gun   127
by Teresa M. Amabile, Constance N. Hadley, and Steven J. Kramer

Strategy Needs Creativity   147
by Adam Brandenburger

How to Build a Culture of Originality   159
by Adam Grant

About the Contributors   175
Index   179

HBR'S 10 MUST READS

On
Creativity

Reclaim Your Creative Confidence

by Tom Kelley and David Kelley

MOST PEOPLE ARE BORN CREATIVE. As children, we revel in imaginary play, ask outlandish questions, draw blobs and call them dinosaurs. But over time, because of socialization and formal education, a lot of us start to stifle those impulses. We learn to be warier of judgment, more cautious, more analytical. The world seems to divide into "creatives" and "noncreatives," and too many people consciously or unconsciously resign themselves to the latter category.

And yet we know that creativity is essential to success in any discipline or industry. According to a recent IBM survey of chief executives around the world, it's the most sought-after trait in leaders today. No one can deny that creative thinking has enabled the rise and continued success of countless companies, from startups like Facebook and Google to stalwarts like Procter & Gamble and General Electric.

Students often come to Stanford University's "d.school" (which was founded by one of us—David Kelley—and is formally known as the Hasso Plattner Institute of Design) to develop their creativity. Clients work with IDEO, our design and innovation consultancy, for the same reason. But along the way, we've learned that our job isn't to *teach* them creativity. It's to help them *rediscover* their creative confidence—the natural ability to come up with new ideas and the courage to try them out. We do this by giving them strategies to get past four fears that hold most of us back: fear of the messy unknown, fear of being judged, fear of the first step, and fear of losing control.

Easier said than done, you might argue. But we know it's possible for people to overcome even their most deep-seated fears. Consider the work of Albert Bandura, a world-renowned psychologist and Stanford professor. In one series of early experiments, he helped people conquer lifelong snake phobias by guiding them through a series of increasingly demanding interactions. They would start by watching a snake through a two-way mirror. Once comfortable with that, they'd progress to observing it through an open door, then to watching someone else touch the snake, then to touching it themselves through a heavy leather glove, and, finally, in a few hours, to touching it with their own bare hands. Bandura calls this process of experiencing one small success after another "guided mastery." The people who went through it weren't just cured of a crippling fear they had assumed was untreatable. They also had less anxiety and more success in other parts of their lives, taking up new and potentially frightening activities like horseback riding and public speaking. They tried harder, persevered longer, and had more resilience in the face of failure. They had gained a new confidence in their ability to attain what they set out to do.

We've used much the same approach over the past 30 years to help people transcend the fears that block their creativity. You break challenges down into small steps and then build confidence by succeeding on one after another. Creativity is something you practice, not just a talent you're born with. The process may feel a little uncomfortable at first, but—as the snake phobics learned—the discomfort quickly fades away and is replaced with new confidence and capabilities.

Fear of the Messy Unknown

Creative thinking in business begins with having empathy for your customers (whether they're internal or external), and you can't get that sitting behind a desk. Yes, we know it's cozy in your office. Everything is reassuringly familiar; information comes

Idea in Brief

Most people are born creative. But over time, a lot of us learn to stifle those impulses. We become warier of judgment, more cautious, more analytical. The world seems to divide into "creatives" and "noncreatives," and too many people resign themselves to the latter category. And yet we know that creativity is essential to success in any discipline or industry.

The good news is that we all can rediscover our creative confidence. The trick is to overcome the four big fears that hold most of us back: fear of the messy unknown, fear of judgment, fear of the first step, and fear of losing control.

This chapter describes an approach based on the work of psychologist Albert Bandura in helping patients get over their snake phobias: You break challenges down into small steps and then build confidence by succeeding on one after another. Creativity is something you practice, not just a talent you are born with.

from predictable sources; contradictory data are weeded out and ignored. Out in the world, it's more chaotic. You have to deal with unexpected findings, with uncertainty, and with irrational people who say things you don't want to hear. But that is where you find insights—and creative breakthroughs. Venturing forth in pursuit of learning, even without a hypothesis, can open you up to new information and help you discover nonobvious needs. Otherwise, you risk simply reconfirming ideas you've already had or waiting for others—your customers, your boss, or even your competitors—to tell you what to do.

At the d.school, we routinely assign students to do this sort of anthropological fieldwork—to get out of their comfort zones and into the world—until, suddenly, they start doing it on their own. Consider a computer scientist, two engineers, and an MBA student, all of whom took the Extreme Affordability class taught by Stanford business school professor Jim Patell. They eventually realized that they couldn't complete their group project—to research and design a low-cost incubator for newborn babies in the developing world—while living in safe, suburban California. So they gathered their courage and visited rural Nepal. Talking with families and doctors firsthand, they learned that the babies in gravest danger were those

Tackling the Mess, One Step at a Time

by Caroline O'Connor and Sarah Stein Greenberg

YOU CAN WORK UP the confidence to tackle the big fears that hold most of us back by starting small. Here are a few ways to get comfortable with venturing into the messy unknown. The list gets increasingly challenging, but you can follow the first two suggestions without even leaving your desk.

Lurk in Online Forums

Listen in as potential customers share information, air grievances, and ask questions—it's the virtual equivalent of hanging around a popular café. You're not looking for evaluations of features or cost; you're searching for clues about their concerns and desires.

Pick Up the Phone and Call Your Own Company's Customer Service Line

Walk through the experience as if you were a customer, noting how your problem is handled and how you're feeling along the way.

Seek Out an Unexpected Expert

What does the receptionist in your building know about your firm's customer experience? If you use a car service for work travel, what insights do the drivers have about your firm? If you're in health care, talk to a medical assistant, not a doctor. If you make a physical product, ask a repair person to tell you about common failure areas.

Act Like a Spy

Take a magazine and a pair of headphones to a store or an industry conference (or, if your customers are internal, a break room or lunch area). Pretend to read while you observe. Watch as if you were a kid, trying to understand what is going on. How are people interacting with your offering? What can you glean from their body language?

Casually Interview a Customer or Potential Customer

After you've gotten more comfortable venturing out, try this: Write down a few open-ended questions about your product or service. Go to a place where your customers tend to gather, find someone you'd be comfortable approaching, and say you'd like to ask a few questions. If the person refuses? No problem, just try someone else. Eventually you'll find someone who's dying to talk to you. Press for more detail with every question. Even if you think you understand, ask "Why is that?" or "Can you tell me more about that?" Get people to dig into their own underlying assumptions.

born prematurely in areas far from hospitals. Nepalese villagers didn't need a cheaper incubator at the hospital—they needed a fail-safe way to keep babies warm when they were away from doctors who could do so effectively. Those insights led the team to design a miniature "sleeping bag" with a pouch containing a special heat-storing wax. The Embrace Infant Warmer costs 99% less than a tra-ditional incubator and can maintain the right temperature for up to six hours without an external power source. The innovation has the potential to save millions of low-birth-weight and premature babies every year, and it came about only because the team members were willing to throw themselves into unfamiliar territory.

Another example comes from two students, Akshay Kothari and Ankit Gupta, who took the d.school's Launchpad course. The class required them to start a company from scratch by the end of the 10-week academic quarter. Both were self-described "geeks"—technically brilliant, deeply analytical, and definitely shy. But they opted to work on their project—an elegant news reader for the then-newly released iPad—off-campus in a Palo Alto café where they'd be surrounded by potential users. Getting over the awkwardness of approaching strangers, Akshay gath-ered feedback by asking café patrons to experiment with his pro-totypes. Ankit coded hundreds of small variations to be tested each day—changing everything from interaction patterns to the size of a button. In a matter of weeks they rapidly iterated their way to a successful product. "We went from people saying, 'This is crap,'" says Akshay, "to 'Is this app preloaded on every iPad?'" The result—Pulse News—received public praise from Steve Jobs at a worldwide developer's conference only a few months later, has been downloaded by 15 million people, and is one of the original 50 apps in Apple's App Store Hall of Fame.

It's not just entrepreneurs and product developers who should get into "the mess." Senior managers also must hear directly from anyone affected by their decisions. For instance, midway through a management off-site IDEO held for ConAgra Foods, the executives broke away from their upscale conference rooms to explore gritty Detroit neighborhoods, where you can go miles without seeing a grocery store. They personally observed how inner-city residents reacted to food products and spoke with an urban farmer who hopes to turn abandoned lots into community gardens. Now, according to Al Bolles, ConAgra's executive vice president of research, quality, and innovation, such behavior is common at the company. "A few years ago, it was hard to pry my executive team away from the office," he says, "but now we venture out and get onto our customers' home turf to get insights about what they really need."

Fear of Being Judged

If the scribbling, singing, dancing kindergartner symbolizes unfettered creative expression, the awkward teenager represents the opposite: someone who cares—*deeply*—about what other people think. It takes only a few years to develop that fear of judgment, but it stays with us throughout our adult lives, often constraining our careers. Most of us accept that when we are learning, say, to ski, others will see us fall down until practice pays off. But we can't risk our business-world ego in the same way. As a result, we self-edit, killing potentially creative ideas because we're afraid our bosses or peers will see us fail. We stick to "safe" solutions or suggestions. We hang back, allowing others to take risks. But you can't be creative if you are constantly censoring yourself.

Half the battle is to resist judging *yourself*. If you can listen to your own intuition and embrace more of your ideas (good and bad), you're already partway to overcoming this fear. So take baby steps, as Bandura's clients did. Instead of letting thoughts run through your head and down the drain, capture them systematically in some form of idea notebook. Keep a whiteboard and marker in the shower. Schedule daily "white space" in your calendar, where your only task is to think or take a walk and daydream. When you try to generate ideas, shoot for 100 instead of 10. Defer your own judgment and you'll be surprised at how many ideas you have—and like—by the end of the week.

Also, try using new language when you give feedback, and encourage your collaborators to do the same. At the d.school, our feedback typically starts with "I like . . ." and moves on to "I wish . . ." instead of just passing judgment with put-downs like "That will never work." Opening with the positives and then using the first person for suggestions signals that "This is just my opinion and I want to help," which makes listeners more receptive to your ideas.

We recently worked with Air New Zealand to reinvent the customer experience for its long-distance flights. As a highly regulated industry, airlines tend toward conservatism. To overcome the cultural norm of skepticism and caution, we started with a workshop aimed at generating crazy ideas. Executives brainstormed and prototyped a dozen unconventional (and some seemingly impractical) concepts, including harnesses that hold people standing up, groups of seats facing one another around a table, and even hammocks and bunk beds. Everyone was doing it, so no one was scared he or she would be judged. This willingness to consider wild notions and defer judgment eventually led the Air New Zealand team to a creative breakthrough: the Skycouch, a lie-flat seat for economy class. At first, it seemed impossible that such a seat could be made without enlarging its footprint (seats in business and first-class cabins take up much more space), but the new design does just that: A heavily padded section swings up like a footrest to transform an airline row into a futon-like platform that a couple can lie down on together. The Skycouch is now featured on a number of Air New Zealand's international flights, and the company has won several industry awards as a result.

Fear of the First Step

Even when we want to embrace our creative ideas, acting on them presents its own challenges. Creative efforts are hardest at the beginning. The writer faces the blank page; the teacher, the start of school; businesspeople, the first day of a new project. In a broader sense, we're also talking about fear of charting a new path or breaking out of your predictable workflow. To overcome this inertia, good ideas are not enough. You need to stop planning and just get started—and the best way to do that is to stop focusing on the huge overall task and find a small piece you can tackle right away.

7

Bestselling writer Anne Lamott expertly captures this idea in a story from her childhood. Her brother had been assigned a school report about birds, but he waited to start on it until the night before it was due. He was near tears, overwhelmed by the task ahead, until his father gave him some wise advice: "Bird by bird, buddy. Just take it bird by bird." In a business context, you can push yourself to take the first step by asking: What is the low-cost experiment? What's the quickest, cheapest way to make progress toward the larger goal?

Or give yourself a crazy deadline, as John Keefe, a d.school alum and a senior editor at radio station WNYC, did after a colleague complained that her mom had to wait at city bus stops never knowing when the next bus would come. If you worked for New York City Transit and your boss asked you to solve that problem, how soon would you promise to get a system up and running? Six weeks? Ten? John, who *doesn't* work for the transit authority, said, "Give me till the end of the day." He bought an 800 number, figured out how to access real-time bus data, and linked it to text-to-speech technology. Within 24 hours, he had set up a service that allowed bus riders to call in, input their bus stop number, and hear the location of the approaching bus. John applies the same fearless attitude to his work at WNYC. "The most effective way I've found to practice design thinking is by showing, not telling," he explains.

Another example of the "start simple" strategy comes from an IDEO project to develop a new dashboard feature for a European luxury car. To test their ideas, designers videotaped an existing car and then used digital effects to layer on proposed features. The rapid prototyping process took less than a week. When the team showed the video to our client, he laughed. "Last time we did something like this," he said, "we built a prototype car, which took almost a year and cost over a million dollars. Then we took a video of it. You skipped the car and went straight to the video."

Our mantra is "Don't get ready, get started!" The first step will seem much less daunting if you make it a tiny one and you force yourself to do it *right now.* Rather than stalling and allowing your anxiety to build, just start inching toward the snake.

Fear of Losing Control

Confidence doesn't simply mean believing your ideas are good. It means having the humility to let go of ideas that aren't working and to accept good ideas from other people. When you abandon the status quo and work collaboratively, you sacrifice control over your product, your team, and your business. But the creative gains can more than compensate. Again, you can start small. If you're facing a tough challenge, try calling a meeting with people fresh to the topic. Or break the routine of a weekly meeting by letting the most junior person in the room set the agenda and lead it. Look for opportunities to cede control and leverage different perspectives.

That's exactly what Bonny Simi, director of airport planning at JetBlue Airways, did after an ice storm closed JFK International Airport for a six-hour stretch in 2007—and disrupted the airline's flight service for the next six days. Everyone knew there were operational problems to be fixed, but no one knew exactly what to do. Fresh from a d.school course, Bonny suggested that JetBlue brainstorm solutions from the bottom up rather than the top down. First, she gathered a team of 120 frontline employees together for just one day—pilots, flight attendants, dispatchers, ramp workers, crew schedulers, and other staff members. Then she mapped out their disruption recovery actions (using yellow Post-it notes) and the challenges they faced (using pink ones). By the end of the day, Bonny's grassroots task force had reached new insights—and resolve. The distributed team then spent the next few months working through more than a thousand pink Post-its to creatively solve each problem. By admitting that the answers lay in the collective, Bonny did more than she could ever have done alone. And JetBlue now recovers from major disruptions significantly faster than it did before.

Our own experience with the open innovation platform OpenIDEO is another case in point. Its launch was scary in two ways: First, we were starting a public conversation that could quickly get out of hand; second, we were admitting that we don't have all the answers. But we were ready, like Bandura's phobics, to take a bigger leap—to touch the snake. And we soon discovered the benefits. Today, the

OpenIDEO community includes about 30,000 people from 170 countries. They may never meet in person, but together they've already made a difference on dozens of initiatives—from helping revitalize cities in economic decline to prototyping ultrasound services for expectant mothers in Colombia. We've learned that no matter what group you're in or where you work, there are always more ideas outside than inside.

For people with backgrounds as diverse as those of Akshay, Ankit, John, and Bonny, fear—of the messy unknown, of judgment, of taking the first step, or of letting go—could have blocked the path to innovation. But instead, they worked to overcome their fears, rediscovered their creative confidence, and made a difference. As Hungarian essayist György Konrád once said, "Courage is only the accumulation of small steps." So don't wait at the starting line. Let go of your fears and begin practicing creative confidence today.

Originally published in December 2012. Reprint R1212K

How to Kill Creativity

by Teresa M. Amabile

WHEN I CONSIDER all the organizations I have studied and worked with over the past 22 years, there can be no doubt: Creativity gets killed much more often than it gets supported. For the most part, this isn't because managers have a vendetta against creativity. On the contrary, most believe in the value of new and useful ideas. However, creativity is undermined unintentionally every day in work environments that were established—for entirely good reasons—to maximize business imperatives such as coordination, productivity, and control.

Managers cannot be expected to ignore business imperatives, of course. But in working toward these imperatives, they may be inadvertently designing organizations that systematically crush creativity. My research shows that it is possible to develop the best of both worlds: organizations in which business imperatives are attended to *and* creativity flourishes. Building such organizations, however, requires us to understand precisely what kinds of managerial practices foster creativity—and which kill it.

What Is Business Creativity?

We tend to associate creativity with the arts and to think of it as the expression of highly original ideas. Think of how Pablo Picasso reinvented the conventions of painting or how William Faulkner redefined fiction. In business, originality isn't enough. To be creative, an idea must also be appropriate—useful and actionable. It must somehow influence the way business gets done—by improving a product, for instance, or by opening up a new way to approach a process.

The associations made between creativity and artistic originality often lead to confusion about the appropriate place of creativity in business organizations. In seminars, I've asked managers if there is any place they *don't* want creativity in their companies. About 80% of the time, they answer, "Accounting." Creativity, they seem to believe, belongs just in marketing and R&D. But creativity can benefit every function of an organization. Think of activity-based accounting. It was an invention—an *accounting* invention—and its impact on business has been positive and profound.

Along with fearing creativity in the accounting department— or really, in any unit that involves systematic processes or legal regulations—many managers also hold a rather narrow view of the creative process. To them, creativity refers to the way people think— how inventively they approach problems, for instance. Indeed, thinking imaginatively is one part of creativity, but two others are also essential: *expertise* and *motivation*.

Expertise encompasses everything that a person knows and can do in the broad domain of his or her work. Take, for example, a scientist at a pharmaceutical company who is charged with developing a blood-clotting drug for hemophiliacs. Her expertise includes her basic talent for thinking scientifically as well as all the knowledge and technical abilities that she has in the fields of medicine, chemistry, biology, and biochemistry. It doesn't matter how she acquired this expertise, whether through formal education, practical experience, or interaction with other professionals. Regardless, her expertise constitutes what the Nobel laureate, economist, and psychologist Herb Simon calls her "network of possible wanderings," the intellectual space that she uses to explore and solve problems. The larger this space, the better.

Creative thinking, as noted above, refers to *how* people approach problems and solutions—their capacity to put existing ideas together in new combinations. The skill itself depends quite a bit on personality as well as on how a person thinks and works. The

Idea in Brief

If the mantra for the current business climate is *Innovate or die*, why do so many companies seem to be choosing the latter option?

Creativity gets killed much more often than it gets supported. The problem is not that managers smother creativity intentionally—the business need for coordination and control can inadvertently undermine employees' ability to put existing ideas together in new and useful ways.

To foster an innovative workplace, you need to pay attention to employees' expertise, creative-thinking skills, and motivation. Of these three, employees' motivation—specifically, their intrinsic motivation, or passion for a certain kind of challenge—is the most potent lever a manager can use to boost creativity *and* his company's future success.

pharmaceutical scientist, for example, will be more creative if her personality is such that she feels comfortable disagreeing with others—that is, if she naturally tries out solutions that depart from the status quo. Her creativity will be enhanced further if she habitually turns problems upside down and combines knowledge from seemingly disparate fields. For example, she might look to botany to help find solutions to the hemophilia problem, using lessons from the vascular systems of plants to spark insights about bleeding in humans.

As for work style, the scientist will be more likely to achieve creative success if she perseveres through a difficult problem. Indeed, plodding through long dry spells of tedious experimentation increases the probability of truly creative breakthroughs. So, too, does a work style that uses "incubation," the ability to set aside difficult problems temporarily, work on something else, and then return later with a fresh perspective.

Expertise and creative thinking are an individual's raw materials—his or her natural resources, if you will. But a third factor—motivation—determines what people will actually do. The scientist can have outstanding educational credentials and a great facility in generating new perspectives to old problems. But if she

Idea in Practice

In business, it isn't enough for an idea to be original—the idea must also be useful, appropriate, and actionable. It must somehow influence the way business gets done—for example, by significantly improving a product or service.

Within every individual, creativity exists as a function of three components:

1. **Expertise** (technical, procedural, and intellectual knowledge). The broader the expertise, the larger the intellectual space a person has to explore and solve problems.

2. **Creative-thinking skills.** These aptitudes, shaped by an individual's personality, determine how flexibly and imaginatively someone approaches problems.

3. **Motivation.** Expertise and creative-thinking skills provide an individual's natural resources for creativity; motivation determines what a person will actually do.

Extrinsic motivation comes from outside the individual—whether it's the offer of a bonus or the threat of firing. Extrinsic motivation doesn't prevent people from being creative, but in many situations it doesn't boost their creativity either. On its own, it can't prompt people to be passionate about their work; in fact, it can lead them to feel bribed or controlled.

Intrinsic motivation, by contrast, comes from inside the individual. It's a person's abiding interest in certain activities or deep love of particular challenges. Employees

lacks the motivation to do a particular job, she simply won't do it; her expertise and creative thinking will either go untapped or be applied to something else.

My research has repeatedly demonstrated, however, that all forms of motivation do not have the same impact on creativity. In fact, it shows that there are two types of motivation—*extrinsic* and *intrinsic*, the latter being far more essential for creativity. But let's explore extrinsic first, because it is often at the root of creativity problems in business.

Extrinsic motivation comes from *outside* a person—whether the motivation is a carrot or a stick. If the scientist's boss promises to reward her financially should the blood-clotting project succeed, or if he threatens to fire her should it fail, she will certainly be motivated are most creative when they are intrinsically motivated—in other words, when the work itself is motivating.

It can be time-consuming to try to influence an employee's expertise or creative-thinking skills. It's easier to affect someone's intrinsic motivation—and the results are more immediate. Activities that enhance intrinsic motivation fall into a few general categories: challenge, freedom, resources, work-group features, supervisory encouragement, and organizational support. Some specific recommendations:

- **Match the right people with the right assignments,** so employees are stretched but not stretched too thin. Work teams that have diverse perspectives will generate more creativity than homogenous groups.

- **Give people freedom within the company's goals.** Tell them which mountain to climb, but let them decide how to climb it. Keep the objectives stable for a meaningful period of time—it's hard to reach the top of a moving mountain.

- **Allocate appropriate amounts of time and project resources.** Organizations routinely kill creativity with fake deadlines—which cause distrust—and impossibly tight ones—which cause burnout.

- **Let employees know that what they do matters.** This will help them sustain their passion for the work.

to find a solution. But this sort of motivation "makes" the scientist do her job in order to get something desirable or avoid something painful.

Obviously, the most common extrinsic motivator managers use is money, which doesn't necessarily stop people from being creative. But in many situations, it doesn't help either, especially when it leads people to feel that they are being bribed or controlled. More important, money by itself doesn't make employees passionate about their jobs. A cash reward can't magically prompt people to find their work interesting if in their hearts they feel it is dull.

But passion and interest—a person's internal desire to do something—are what intrinsic motivation is all about. For instance, the scientist in our example would be intrinsically motivated if her work on the blood-clotting drug was sparked by an intense interest in hemophilia, a personal sense of challenge, or a drive to crack a problem that no one else has been able to solve. When people are intrinsically motivated, they engage in their work for the challenge and enjoyment of it. The work *itself* is motivating. In fact, in our creativity research, my students, colleagues, and I have found so much evidence in favor of intrinsic motivation that we have articulated what we call the *Intrinsic Motivation Principle of Creativity:* People will be most creative when they feel motivated primarily by the interest, satisfaction, and challenge of the work itself—and not by external pressures. (For more on the differences between intrinsic and extrinsic motivation, see the sidebar "The Creativity Maze.")

Managing Creativity

Managers can influence all three components of creativity: expertise, creative-thinking skills, and motivation. But the fact is that the first two are more difficult and time-consuming to influence than motivation. Yes, regular scientific seminars and professional conferences will undoubtedly add to the scientist's expertise in hemophilia and related fields. And training in brainstorming, problem solving, and so-called lateral thinking might give her some new tools to use in tackling the job. But the time and money involved in broadening her knowledge and expanding her creative-thinking skills would be great. By contrast, our research has shown that intrinsic motivation can be increased considerably by even subtle changes in an organization's environment. That is not to say that managers should give up on improving expertise and creative-thinking skills. But when it comes to pulling levers, they should know that those that affect intrinsic motivation will yield more immediate results.

More specifically, then, what managerial practices affect creativity? They fall into six general categories: challenge, freedom, resources, work-group features, supervisory encouragement, and organizational support. These categories have emerged from more than two decades of research focused primarily on one question: What are the links between work environment and creativity? We

The Creativity Maze

TO UNDERSTAND THE DIFFERENCES between extrinsic and intrinsic motivation, imagine a business problem as a maze.

One person might be motivated to make it through the maze as quickly and safely as possible in order to get a tangible reward, such as money—the same way a mouse would rush through for a piece of cheese. This person would look for the simplest, most straightforward path and then take it. In fact, if he is in a real rush to get that reward, he might just take the most beaten path and solve the problem exactly as it has been solved before.

That approach, based on extrinsic motivation, will indeed get him out of the maze. But the solution that arises from the process is likely to be unimaginative. It won't provide new insights about the nature of the problem or reveal new ways of looking at it. The rote solution probably won't move the business forward.

Another person might have a different approach to the maze. She might actually find the process of wandering around the different paths—the challenge and exploration itself—fun and intriguing. No doubt, this journey will take longer and include mistakes, because any maze—any truly complex problem—has many more dead ends than exits. But when the intrinsically motivated person finally does find a way out of the maze—a solution—it very likely will be more interesting than the rote algorithm. It will be more creative.

There is abundant evidence of strong intrinsic motivation in the stories of widely recognized creative people. When asked what makes the difference between creative scientists and those who are less creative, the Nobel prize-winning physicist Arthur Schawlow said, "The labor-of-love aspect is important. The most successful scientists often are not the most talented, but the ones who are just impelled by curiosity. They've got to know what the answer is." Albert Einstein talked about intrinsic motivation as "the enjoyment of seeing and searching." The novelist John Irving, in discussing the very long hours he put into his writing, said, "The unspoken factor is love. The reason I can work so hard at my writing is that it's not work for me." And Michael Jordan, perhaps the most creative basketball player ever, had a "love of the game" clause inserted into his contract; he insisted that he be free to play pick-up basketball games any time he wished.

Creative people are rarely superstars like Michael Jordan. Indeed, most of the creative work done in the business world today gets done by people whose names will never be recorded in history books. They are people with expertise, good creative-thinking skills, and high levels of intrinsic motivation. And just as important, they work in organizations where managers consciously build environments that support these characteristics instead of destroying them.

have used three methodologies: experiments, interviews, and surveys. While controlled experiments allowed us to identify causal links, the interviews and surveys gave us insight into the richness and complexity of creativity within business organizations. We have studied dozens of companies and, within those, hundreds of individuals and teams. In each research initiative, our goal has been to identify which managerial practices are definitively linked to positive creative outcomes and which are not.

For instance, in one project, we interviewed dozens of employees from a wide variety of companies and industries and asked them to describe in detail the most and least creative events in their careers. We then closely studied the transcripts of those interviews, noting the managerial practices—or other patterns—that appeared repeatedly in the successful creativity stories and, conversely, in those that were unsuccessful. Our research has also been bolstered by a quantitative survey instrument called KEYS. Taken by employees at any level of an organization, KEYS consists of 78 questions used to assess various workplace conditions, such as the level of support for creativity from top-level managers or the organization's approach to evaluation.

Taking the six categories that have emerged from our research in turn, let's explore what managers can do to enhance creativity—and what often happens instead. Again, it is important to note that creativity-killing practices are seldom the work of lone managers. Such practices usually are systemic—so widespread that they are rarely questioned.

Challenge

Of all the things managers can do to stimulate creativity, perhaps the most efficacious is the deceptively simple task of matching people with the right assignments. Managers can match people with jobs that play to their expertise and their skills in creative thinking, *and* ignite intrinsic motivation. Perfect matches stretch employees' abilities. The amount of stretch, however, is crucial: not so little that they feel bored but not so much that they feel overwhelmed and threatened by a loss of control.

Making a good match requires that managers possess rich and detailed information about their employees and the available assignments. Such information is often difficult and time-consuming to gather. Perhaps that's why good matches are so rarely made. In fact, one of the most common ways managers kill creativity is by not trying to obtain the information necessary to make good connections between people and jobs. Instead, something of a shotgun wedding occurs. The most eligible employee is wed to the most eligible—that is, the most urgent and open—assignment. Often, the results are predictably unsatisfactory for all involved.

Freedom
When it comes to granting freedom, the key to creativity is giving people autonomy concerning the means—that is, concerning process—but not necessarily the ends. People will be more creative, in other words, if you give them freedom to decide how to climb a particular mountain. You needn't let them choose which mountain to climb. In fact, clearly specified strategic goals often enhance people's creativity.

I'm not making the case that managers should leave their subordinates entirely out of goal- or agenda-setting discussions. But they should understand that inclusion in those discussions will not necessarily enhance creative output and certainly will not be sufficient to do so. It is far more important that whoever sets the goals also makes them clear to the organization and that these goals remain stable for a meaningful period of time. It is difficult, if not impossible, to work creatively toward a target if it keeps moving.

Autonomy around process fosters creativity because giving people freedom in how they approach their work heightens their intrinsic motivation and sense of ownership. Freedom about process also allows people to approach problems in ways that make the most of their expertise and their creative-thinking skills. The task may end up being a stretch for them, but they can use their strengths to meet the challenge.

How do executives mismanage freedom? There are two common ways. First, managers tend to change goals frequently or fail to define them clearly. Employees may have freedom around process, but if they don't know where they are headed, such freedom is pointless. And second, some managers fall short on this dimension by granting autonomy in name only. They claim that employees are "empowered" to explore the maze as they search for solutions, but, in fact, the process is proscribed. Employees diverge at their own risk.

Resources

The two main resources that affect creativity are time and money. Managers need to allot these resources carefully. Like matching people with the right assignments, deciding how much time and money to give to a team or project is a sophisticated judgment call that can either support or kill creativity.

Consider time. Under some circumstances, time pressure can heighten creativity. Say, for instance, that a competitor is about to launch a great product at a lower price than your offering or that society faces a serious problem and desperately needs a solution—such as an AIDS vaccine. In such situations, both the time crunch and the importance of the work legitimately make people feel that they must rush. Indeed, cases like these would be apt to increase intrinsic motivation by increasing the sense of challenge.

Organizations routinely kill creativity with fake deadlines or impossibly tight ones. The former create distrust and the latter cause burnout. In either case, people feel overcontrolled and unfulfilled—which invariably damages motivation. Moreover, creativity often takes time. It can be slow going to explore new concepts, put together unique solutions, and wander through the maze. Managers who do not allow time for exploration or do not schedule in incubation periods are unwittingly standing in the way of the creative process.

When it comes to project resources, again managers must make a fit. They must determine the funding, people, and other resources that a team legitimately needs to complete an assignment—and they must know how much the organization can legitimately afford to allocate to the assignment. Then they must strike a compromise.

Interestingly, adding more resources above a "threshold of suffi-ciency" does not boost creativity. Below that threshold, however, a restriction of resources can dampen creativity. Unfortunately, many managers don't realize this and therefore often make another mistake. They keep resources tight, which pushes people to chan-nel their creativity into finding additional resources, not in actually developing new products or services.

Another resource that is misunderstood when it comes to creativ-ity is physical space. It is almost conventional wisdom that creative teams need open, comfortable offices. Such an atmosphere won't hurt creativity, and it may even help, but it is not nearly as impor-tant as other managerial initiatives that influence creativity. Indeed, a problem we have seen time and time again is managers paying attention to creating the "right" physical space at the expense of more high-impact actions, such as matching people to the right assignments and granting freedom around work processes.

Work-group features

If you want to build teams that come up with creative ideas, you must pay careful attention to the design of such teams. That is, you must create mutually supportive groups with a diversity of perspec-tives and backgrounds. Why? Because when teams comprise people with various intellectual foundations and approaches to work—that is, different expertise and creative thinking styles—ideas often com-bine and combust in exciting and useful ways.

Diversity, however, is only a starting point. Managers must also make sure that the teams they put together have three other fea-tures. First, the members must share excitement over the team's goal. Second, members must display a willingness to help their teammates through difficult periods and setbacks. And third, every member must recognize the unique knowledge and perspective that other members bring to the table. These factors enhance not only intrinsic motivation but also expertise and creative-thinking skills.

Again, creating such teams requires managers to have a deep understanding of their people. They must be able to assess them not just for their knowledge but for their attitudes about potential fellow team members and the collaborative process, for their problem-solving styles, and for their motivational hot buttons. Putting together a team with just the right chemistry—just the right level of diversity and supportiveness—can be difficult, but our research shows how powerful it can be.

It follows, then, that one common way managers kill creativity is by assembling homogeneous teams. The lure to do so is great. Homogeneous teams often reach "solutions" more quickly and with less friction along the way. These teams often report high morale, too. But homogeneous teams do little to enhance expertise and creative thinking. Everyone comes to the table with a similar mindset. They leave with the same.

Supervisory encouragement

Most managers are extremely busy. They are under pressure for results. It is therefore easy for them to let praise for creative efforts—not just creative successes but unsuccessful efforts, too—fall by the wayside. One very simple step managers can take to foster creativity is to not let that happen.

The connection to intrinsic motivation here is clear. Certainly, people can find their work interesting or exciting without a cheering section—for some period of time. But to *sustain* such passion, most people need to feel as if their work matters to the organization or to some important group of people. Otherwise, they might as well do their work at home and for their own personal gain.

Managers in successful, creative organizations rarely offer specific extrinsic rewards for particular outcomes. However, they freely and generously recognize creative work by individuals and teams—often before the ultimate commercial impact of those efforts is known. By contrast, managers who kill creativity do so either by failing to acknowledge innovative efforts or by greeting them with skepticism. In many companies, for instance, new ideas are met not with open minds but with time-consuming layers of evaluation—or even with harsh criticism. When someone suggests a new product or process, senior managers take weeks to respond. Or they put that person through an excruciating critique.

Not every new idea is worthy of consideration, of course, but in many organizations, managers habitually demonstrate a reaction that damages creativity. They look for reasons to not use a new idea instead of searching for reasons to explore it further. An interesting psychological dynamic underlies this phenomenon. Our research shows that people believe that they will appear smarter to their bosses if they are more critical—and it often works. In many organizations, it is professionally rewarding to react critically to new ideas.

Unfortunately, this sort of negativity bias can have severe consequences for the creativity of those being evaluated. How? First, a culture of evaluation leads people to focus on the external rewards and punishments associated with their output, thus increasing the presence of extrinsic motivation and its potentially negative effects on intrinsic motivation. Second, such a culture creates a climate of fear, which again undermines intrinsic motivation.

Finally, negativity also shows up in how managers treat people whose ideas don't pan out: Often, they are terminated or otherwise warehoused within the organization. Of course, ultimately, ideas do need to work; remember that creative ideas in business must be new *and* useful. The dilemma is that you can't possibly know beforehand which ideas will pan out. Furthermore, dead ends can sometimes be very enlightening. In many business situations, knowing what doesn't work can be as useful as knowing what does. But if people do not perceive any "failure value" for projects that ultimately do not achieve commercial success, they'll become less and less likely to experiment, explore, and connect with their work on a personal level. Their intrinsic motivation will evaporate.

Supervisory encouragement comes in other forms besides rewards and punishment. Another way managers can support creativity is to serve as role models, persevering through tough problems as well as encouraging collaboration and communication within the team. Such behavior enhances all three components of the creative process, and it has the added virtue of being a high-impact practice that a single manager can take on his or her own. It is better still when all managers in an organization serve as role models for the attitudes and behaviors that encourage and nurture creativity.

Organizational support

Encouragement from supervisors certainly fosters creativity, but creativity is truly enhanced when the entire organization supports it. Such support is the job of an organization's leaders, who must put in place appropriate systems or procedures and emphasize values that make it clear that creative efforts are a top priority. For example, creativity-supporting organizations consistently reward creativity, but they avoid using money to "bribe" people to come up with innovative ideas. Because monetary rewards make people feel as if they are being controlled, such a tactic probably won't work. At the same time, not providing sufficient recognition and rewards for creativity can spawn negative feelings within an organization. People can feel used, or at the least underappreciated, for their creative efforts. And it is rare to find the energy and passion of intrinsic motivation coupled with resentment.

Most important, an organization's leaders can support creativity by mandating information sharing and collaboration and by ensuring that political problems do not fester. Information sharing and collaboration support all three components of creativity. Take expertise. The more often people exchange ideas and data by working together, the more knowledge they will have. The same dynamic can be said for creative thinking. In fact, one way to enhance the creative thinking of employees is to expose them to various approaches to problem solving. With the exception of hardened misanthropes, information sharing and collaboration heighten peoples' enjoyment of work and thus their intrinsic motivation.

Whether or not you are seeking to enhance creativity, it is probably never a good idea to let political problems fester in an organizational setting. Infighting, politicking, and gossip are particularly damaging to creativity because they take peoples' attention away from work. That sense of mutual purpose and excitement so central to intrinsic motivation invariably lessens when people are cliquish or at war with one another. Indeed, our research suggests that intrinsic motivation increases when people are aware that those around them are excited by their jobs. When political problems abound, people feel that their work is threatened by others' agendas.

Finally, politicking also undermines expertise. The reason? Politics get in the way of open communication, obstructing the flow of information from point A to point B. Knowledge stays put and expertise suffers.

From the Individual to the Organization

Can executives build entire organizations that support creativity? The answer is yes. Consider the results of an intensive research project we recently completed called the Team Events Study. Over the course of two years, we studied more than two dozen teams in seven companies across three industries: high tech, consumer products, and chemicals. By following each team every day through the entire course of a creative project, we had a window into the details of what happened as the project progressed—or failed to progress, as the case may be. We did this through daily confidential email reports from every person on each of the teams. At the end of each project, and at several points along the way, we used confidential reports from company experts and from team members to assess the level of creativity used in problem solving as well as the overall success of the project.

As might be expected, the teams and the companies varied widely in how successful they were at producing creative work. One organization, which I will call Chemical Central Research, seemed to be a veritable hotbed of creativity. Chemical Central supplied its parent organization with new formulations for a wide variety of industrial and consumer products. In many respects, however, members of Chemical Central's development teams were unremarkable. They were well educated, but no more so than people in many other companies we had studied. The company was doing well financially, but not enormously better than most other companies. What seemed to distinguish this organization was the quality of leadership at both the top-management level and the team level. The way managers formed teams, communicated with them, and supported their work enabled them to establish an organization in which creativity was continually stimulated.

The three components of creativity

Within every individual, creativity is a function of three components: expertise, creative-thinking skills, and motivation. Can managers influence these components? The answer is an emphatic yes—for better or for worse—through workplace practices and conditions.

Expertise is, in a word, knowledge—technical, procedural, and intellectual.

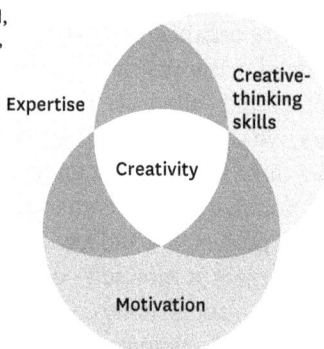

Creative-thinking skills determine how flexibly and imaginatively people approach problems. Do their solutions upend the status quo? Do they persevere through dry spells?

Expertise

Creative-thinking skills

Creativity

Motivation

Not all **motivation** is created equal. An inner passion to solve the problem at hand leads to solutions far more creative than do external rewards, such as money. This component—called *intrinsic motivation*—is the one that can be most immediately influenced by the work environment.

We saw managers making excellent matches between people and assignments again and again at Chemical Central. On occasion, team members were initially unsure of whether they were up to the challenge they were given. Almost invariably, though, they found their passion and interest growing through a deep involvement in the work. Their managers knew to match them with jobs that had them working at the top of their competency levels, pushing the frontiers of their skills, and developing new competencies. But managers were careful not to allow too big a gap between employees' assignments and their abilities.

Moreover, managers at Chemical Central collaborated with the teams from the outset of a project to clarify goals. The final goals, however, were set by the managers. Then, at the day-to-day operational level, the teams were given a great deal of autonomy to make their own decisions about product development. Throughout the project, the teams' leaders and top-level managers periodically checked to see that work was directed toward the overall goals. But people were given real freedom around the implementation of the goals.

As for work-group design, every Chemical Central team, though relatively small (between four and nine members), included members of diverse professional and ethnic backgrounds. Occasionally, that diversity led to communication difficulties. But more often, it sparked new insights and allowed the teams to come up with a wider variety of ways to accomplish their goals.

One team, for example, was responsible for devising a new way to make a major ingredient for one of the company's most important products. Because managers at Chemical Central had worked consciously to create a diverse team, it happened that one member had both a legal and a technical background. This person realized that the team might well be able to patent its core idea, giving the company a clear advantage in a new market. Because team members were mutually supportive, that member was willing and eager to work closely with the inventor. Together, these individuals helped the team navigate its way through the patent application process. The team was successful and had fun along the way.

Supervisory encouragement and organizational support were also widespread at Chemical Central. For instance, a member of one team received a company award as an outstanding scientist even though, along the way, he had experienced many failures as well as successes. At one point, after spending a great deal of time on one experiment, he told us, "All I came up with was a pot of junk." Still, the company did not punish or warehouse him because of a creative effort that had failed. Instead, he was publicly lauded for his consistently creative work.

Finally, Chemical Central's leaders did much to encourage teams to seek support from all units within their divisions and to encourage collaboration across all quarters. The general manager of the research unit himself set an example, offering both strategic and technical ideas whenever teams approached him for help. Indeed, he explicitly made cross-team support a priority among top scientists in the organization. As a result, such support was expected and recognized.

For example, one team was about to test a new formulation for one of the company's major products. Because the team was small, it had to rely on a materials-analysis group within the organization to help conduct the tests. The analysis group not only helped out but also set aside generous blocks of time during the week before testing to help the team understand the nature and limits of the information the group would provide, when they would have it, and what they would need from the team to support them effectively. Members of the team were confident that they could rely on the materials-analysis group throughout the process, and the trials went well—despite the usual technical difficulties encountered in such testing.

By contrast, consider what we observed at another company in our study, a consumer products company we'll call National Houseware Products. For years, National had been well known for its innovation. But recently, the company had been restructured to accommodate a major growth spurt, and many senior managers had been fired or transferred. National's work environment had undergone drastic changes. At the same time, new product successes and new business ideas seemed to be slowing to a trickle. Interestingly, the daily reports of the Team Events Study revealed that virtually all creativity killers were present.

Managers undermined autonomy by continually changing goals and interfering with processes. At one quarterly review meeting, for example, four priorities that had been defined by management at the previous quarterly review meeting were not even mentioned. In another instance, a product that had been identified as the team's number one project was suddenly dropped without explanation.

Resources were similarly mismanaged. For instance, management perennially put teams under severe and seemingly arbitrary time and resource constraints. At first, many team members were energized by the fire-fighting atmosphere. They threw themselves into their work and rallied. But after a few months, their verve had diminished, especially because the pressures had proved meaningless.

But perhaps National's managers damaged creativity most with their approach to evaluation. They were routinely critical of new suggestions. One employee told us that he was afraid to tell his managers about some radical ideas that he had developed to grow his area of the business. The employee was wildly enthusiastic about the potential for his ideas but ultimately didn't mention them to any of his bosses. He wondered why he should bother talking about new ideas when each one was studied for all its flaws instead of its potential. Through its actions, management had too often sent the message that any big ideas about how to change the status quo would be carefully scrutinized. Those individuals brave enough to suggest new ideas had to endure long—often nasty—meetings, replete with suspicious questions.

In another example, when a team took a new competitive pricing program to the boss, it was told that a discussion of the idea would have to wait another month. One exasperated team member noted, "We analyze so long, we've lost the business before we've taken any action at all!"

Yet another National team had put in particularly long hours over a period of several weeks to create a radically improved version of a major product. The team succeeded in bringing out the product on time and in budget, and it garnered promising market response. But management acted as if everything were business as usual, providing no recognition or reward to the team. A couple of months later, when we visited the team to report the results of our study, we learned that the team leader had just accepted a job from a smaller competitor. He confided that although he felt that the opportunities for advancement and ultimate visibility may have been greater at National, he believed his work and his ideas would be valued more highly somewhere else.

And finally, the managers at National allowed political problems to fester. Consider the time a National team came up with a great idea to save money in manufacturing a new product—which was especially urgent because a competitor had just come out with a similar product at a lower price. The plan was nixed. As a matter of "policy"—a code word for long-held allegiances and rivalries within the company—the manufacturing division wouldn't allow it. One team member commented, "If facts and figures instead of politics reigned supreme, this would be a no-brainer. There are no definable cost savings from running the products where they do, and there is no counterproposal on how to save the money another way. It's just 'No!' because this is the way they want it."

Great Rewards and Risks

The important lesson of the National and Chemical Central stories is that fostering creativity is in the hands of managers as they think about, design, and establish the work environment. Creativity often requires that managers radically change the ways in which they build and interact with work groups. In many respects, it calls for a conscious culture change. But it can be done, and the rewards can be great.

The risks of not doing so may be even greater. When creativity is killed, an organization loses a potent competitive weapon: new ideas. It can also lose the energy and commitment of its people. Indeed, in all my years of research into creativity, perhaps the most difficult part has been hearing people complain that they feel stifled, frustrated, and shut down by their organizations. As one team member at National told us, "By the time I get home every day, I feel physically, emotionally, and intellectually drained. Help!"

Even if organizations seemed trapped in organizational ecosystems that kill creativity—as in the case of National Houseware Products—it is still possible to effect widespread change. Consider a recent transformation at Procter & Gamble. Once a hotbed of creativity, P&G had in recent years seen the number of its product innovations decline significantly. In response, the company established Corporate New Ventures (CNV), a small cross-functional team that embodies many of the creativity-enhancing practices described in this article.

In terms of challenge, for instance, members of the CNV team were allowed to elect themselves. How better to make sure someone is intrinsically motivated for an assignment than to ask for volunteers? Building a team from volunteers, it should be noted, was a major departure from standard P&G procedures. Members of the CNV team also were given a clear, challenging strategic goal: to invent radical new products that would build the company's future. Again departing from typical P&G practices, the team was given enormous latitude around how, when, and where they approached their work.

The list of how CNV broke with P&G's creativity-killing practices is a long one. On nearly every creativity-support dimension in the KEYS work-environment survey, CNV scored higher than national norms and higher than the pre-CNV environment at P&G. But more important than the particulars is the question: Has the changed environment resulted in more creative work? Undeniably so, and the evidence is convincing. In the three years since its inception, CNV has handed off 11 projects to the business sectors for execution. And as of early 1998, those products were beginning to flow out of the pipeline. The first product, designed to provide portable heat for several hours' relief of minor pain, was already in test marketing. And six other products were slated to go to test market within a year. Not surprisingly, given CNV's success, P&G is beginning to expand both the size and the scope of its CNV venture.

Even if you believe that your organization fosters creativity, take a hard look for creativity killers. Some of them may be flourishing in a dark corner—or even in the light. But rooting out creativity-killing behaviors isn't enough. You have to make a conscious effort to support creativity. The result can be a truly innovative company where creativity doesn't just survive but actually thrives.

Originally published in September–October 1998. Reprint 98501

How Pixar Fosters Collective Creativity

by Ed Catmull

A FEW YEARS AGO, I had lunch with the head of a major motion picture studio, who declared that his central problem was not finding good people—it was finding good ideas. Since then, when giving talks, I've asked audiences whether they agree with him. Almost always there's a 50/50 split, which has astounded me because I couldn't disagree more with the studio executive. His belief is rooted in a misguided view of creativity that exaggerates the importance of the initial idea in creating an original product. And it reflects a profound misunderstanding of how to manage the large risks inherent in producing breakthroughs.

When it comes to producing breakthroughs, both technological and artistic, Pixar's track record is unique. In the early 1990s, we were known as the leading technological pioneer in the field of computer animation. Our years of R&D culminated in the release of *Toy Story* in 1995, the world's first computer-animated feature film. In the following 13 years, we have released eight other films (*A Bug's Life; Toy Story 2; Monsters, Inc.; Finding Nemo; The Incredibles; Cars; Ratatouille;* and *WALL-E*), which also have been blockbusters. Unlike most other studios, we have never bought scripts or movie ideas from the outside. All of our stories, worlds, and characters were created internally by our community of artists. And in making these films, we have continued to push the technological boundaries of computer animation, securing dozens of patents in the process.

While I'm not foolish enough to predict that we will never have a flop, I don't think our success is largely luck. Rather, I believe our adherence to a set of principles and practices for managing creative talent and risk is responsible. Pixar is a community in the true sense of the word. We think that lasting relationships matter, and we share some basic beliefs: Talent is rare. Management's job is not to prevent risk but to build the capability to recover when failures occur. It must be safe to tell the truth. We must constantly challenge all of our assumptions and search for the flaws that could destroy our culture. In the last two years, we've had a chance to test whether our principles and practices are transferable. After Pixar's 2006 merger with the Walt Disney Company, its CEO, Bob Iger, asked me, chief creative officer John Lasseter, and other Pixar senior managers to help him revive Disney Animation Studios. The success of our efforts prompted me to share my thinking on how to build a sustainable creative organization.

What Is Creativity?

People tend to think of creativity as a mysterious solo act, and they typically reduce products to a single idea: This is a movie about toys, or dinosaurs, or love, they'll say. However, in filmmaking and many other kinds of complex product development, creativity involves a large number of people from different disciplines working effectively together to solve a great many problems. The initial idea for the movie—what people in the movie business call "the high concept"—is merely one step in a long, arduous process that takes four to five years.

A movie contains literally tens of thousands of ideas. They're in the form of every sentence; in the performance of each line; in the design of characters, sets, and backgrounds; in the locations of the camera; in the colors, the lighting, the pacing. The director and the other creative leaders of a production do not come up with all the ideas on their own; rather, every single member of the 200- to 250-person production group makes suggestions. Creativity must be present at every level of every artistic and technical part of the organization.

Idea in Brief

A robot falls in love in a post-apocalyptic world. A French rat sets out to become a chef. A suburban family of superheroes defeats a power-hungry villain. Unexpected ideas, all—yet Pixar Animation Studios is turning these and other novel ideas into block-buster films.

How? As Catmull explains, Pixar's leaders have discovered potent practices for structuring and oper-ating a creative organization. For example, they give writers, artists, and other "creatives" enormous leeway to make decisions. They

make it safe for people to share unfinished work with peers, who provide candid feedback. And they conduct project postmortems in ways that extract the most valuable lessons for mitigating risk on subsequent projects.

The effort has paid off. Pixar has racked up a unique track record of success: It's the leading pioneer in computer animation. It has never had to buy scripts or movie ideas from outside. And since 1995, it has released seven films—all of which became huge hits.

The leaders sort through a mass of ideas to find the ones that fit into a coherent whole—that support the story—which is a very difficult task. It's like an archaeological dig where you don't know what you're looking for or whether you will even find anything. The process is downright scary.

Then again, if we aren't always at least a little scared, we're not doing our job. We're in a business whose customers want to see something new every time they go to the theater. This means we have to put ourselves at great risk. Our most recent film, *WALL-E*, is a robot love story set in a post-apocalyptic world full of trash. And our previous movie, *Ratatouille*, is about a French rat who aspires to be a chef. Talk about unexpected ideas! At the outset of making these movies, we simply didn't know if they would work. However, since we're supposed to offer something that isn't obvious, we bought into somebody's initial vision and took a chance.

To act in this fashion, we as executives have to resist our natural tendency to avoid or minimize risks, which, of course, is much easier said than done. In the movie business and plenty of others, this instinct leads executives to choose to copy successes rather than try to create something brand-new. That's why you see so many movies

Idea in Practice

Catmull suggests these principles for managing your creative organization:

Empower your creatives. Give your creative people control over every stage of idea development.

Example:

At most studios, a specialized development department generates new movie ideas. Pixar assembles cross-company teams for this purpose. Teams comprise directors, writers, artists, and storyboard people who originate and refine ideas until they have potential to become great films. The development department's job? Find people who'll work effectively together. Ensure healthy social dynamics in the team. Help the team solve problems.

Create a peer culture. Encourage people throughout your company to help one another produce their best work.

Example:

At Pixar, daily animation work is shown in an incomplete state to the whole crew. This process helps people get over any embarrassment about sharing unfinished work—so they become even more creative. It enables creative leads to communicate important points to the entire crew at once. And it's inspiring: A highly innovative piece of animation sparks others to raise their game.

Free up communication. The most efficient way to resolve the numerous problems that arise in any complex project is to trust people to address difficulties directly, without having to get permission. So, give everyone the freedom to communicate with anyone.

that are so much alike. It also explains why a lot of films aren't very good. If you want to be original, you have to accept the uncertainty, even when it's uncomfortable, and have the capability to recover when your organization takes a big risk and fails. What's the key to being able to recover? Talented people! Contrary to what the studio head asserted at lunch that day, such people are not so easy to find.

What's equally tough, of course, is getting talented people to work effectively with one another. That takes trust and respect, which we as managers can't mandate; they must be earned over time. What we can do is construct an environment that nurtures trusting and respectful relationships and unleashes everyone's creativity. If we get that right, the result is a vibrant community where talented people are loyal to

Example:

Within Pixar, members of any department can approach anyone in another department to solve problems, without having to go through "proper" channels. Managers understand they don't always have to be the first to know about something going on in their realm, and that it's okay to walk into a meeting and be surprised.

Craft a learning environment. Reinforce the mindset that you're all learning—and it's fun to learn together.

Example:

"Pixar University" trains people in multiple skills as they advance in their careers. It also offers optional courses (screenplay writing, drawing, sculpting) so that people from different disciplines can interact and appreciate what each other does.

Get more out of postmortems. Many people dislike project postmortems. They'd rather talk about what went right than what went wrong. And after investing extensive time on the project, they'd like to move on. Structure your postmortems to stimulate discussion.

Example:

Pixar asks postmortem participants to list the top five things they'd do again and the top five they wouldn't do. The positive-negative balance makes it a safer environment to explore every aspect of the project. Participants also bring in lots of performance data—including metrics such as how often something had to be reworked. Data further stimulates discussion and challenges assumptions based on subjective impressions.

one another and their collective work, everyone feels that they are part of something extraordinary, and their passion and accomplishments make the community a magnet for talented people coming out of schools or working at other places. I know what I'm describing is the antithesis of the free-agency practices that prevail in the movie industry, but that's the point: I believe that community matters.

The Roots of Our Culture

My conviction that smart people are more important than good ideas probably isn't surprising. I've had the good fortune to work alongside amazing people in places that pioneered computer graphics.

At the University of Utah, my fellow graduate students included Jim Clark, who cofounded Silicon Graphics and Netscape; John Warnock, who cofounded Adobe; and Alan Kay, who developed object-oriented programming. We had ample funding (thanks to the U.S. Defense Department's Advanced Research Projects Agency), the professors gave us free rein, and there was an exhilarating and creative exchange of ideas.

At the New York Institute of Technology, where I headed a new computer-animation laboratory, one of my first hires was Alvy Ray Smith, who made breakthroughs in computer painting. That made me realize that it's OK to hire people who are smarter than you are.

Then George Lucas, of *Star Wars* fame, hired me to head a major initiative at Lucasfilm to bring computer graphics and other digital technology into films and, later, games. It was thrilling to do research within a film company that was pushing the boundaries. George didn't try to lock up the technology for himself and allowed us to continue to publish and maintain strong academic contacts. This made it possible to attract some of the best people in the industry, including John Lasseter, then an animator from Disney, who was excited by the new possibilities of computer animation.

Last but not least, there's Pixar, which began its life as an independent company in 1986, when Steve Jobs bought the computer division from Lucasfilm, allowing us to pursue our dream of producing computer-animated movies. Steve gave backbone to our desire for excellence and helped us form a remarkable management team. I'd like to think that Pixar captures what's best about all the places I've worked. A number of us have stuck together for decades, pursuing the dream of making computer-animated films, and we still have the pleasure of working together today.

It was only when Pixar experienced a crisis during the production of *Toy Story 2* that my views on how to structure and operate a creative organization began to crystallize. In 1996, while we were working on *A Bug's Life*, our second movie, we started to make a sequel to *Toy Story*. We had enough technical leaders to start a second production, but all of our proven creative leaders—the people who had made *Toy Story*, including John, who was its director; writer Andrew

Stanton; editor Lee Unkrich; and the late Joe Ranft, the movie's head of story—were working on *A Bug's Life*. So we had to form a new creative team of people who had never headed a movie production. We felt this was OK. After all, John, Andrew, Lee, and Joe had never led a full-length animated film production before *Toy Story*.

Disney, which at that time was distributing and cofinancing our films, initially encouraged us to make *Toy Story 2* as a "direct to video"—a movie that would be sold only as home videos and not shown first in theaters. This was Disney's model for keeping alive the characters of successful films, and the expectation was that both the cost and quality would be lower. We realized early on, however, that having two different standards of quality in the same studio was bad for our souls, and Disney readily agreed that the sequel should be a theatrical release. The creative leadership, though, remained the same, which turned out to be a problem.

In the early stage of making a movie, we draw storyboards (a comic-book version of the story) and then edit them together with dialogue and temporary music. These are called story reels. The first versions are very rough, but they give a sense of what the problems are, which in the beginning of all productions are many. We then iterate, and each version typically gets better and better. In the case of *Toy Story 2*, we had a good initial idea for a story, but the reels were not where they ought to have been by the time we started animation, and they were not improving. Making matters worse, the directors and producers were not pulling together to rise to the challenge.

Finally *A Bug's Life* was finished, freeing up John, Andrew, Lee, and Joe to take over the creative leadership of *Toy Story 2*. Given where the production was at that point, 18 months would have been an aggressive schedule, but by then we had only eight left to deliver the film. Knowing that the company's future depended on them, crew members worked at an incredible rate. In the end, with the new leadership, they pulled it off.

How did John and his team save the movie? The problem was not the original core concept, which they retained. The main character, a cowboy doll named Woody, is kidnapped by a toy collector who intends to ship him to a toy museum in Japan. At a critical point

39

in the story, Woody has to decide whether to go to Japan or try to escape and go back to Andy, the boy who owned him. Well, since the movie is coming from Pixar and Disney, you know he's going to end up back with Andy. And if you can easily predict what's going to happen, you don't have any drama. So the challenge was to get the audience to believe that Woody might make a different choice. The first team couldn't figure out how to do it.

John, Andrew, Lee, and Joe solved that problem by adding several elements to show the fears toys might have that people could relate to. One is a scene they created called "Jessie's story." Jessie is a cowgirl doll who is going to be shipped to Japan with Woody. She wants to go, and she explains why to Woody. The audience hears her story in the emotional song "When She Loved Me": She had been the darling of a little girl, but the girl grew up and discarded her. The reality is kids do grow up, life does change, and sometimes you have to move on. Since the audience members know the truth of this, they can see that Woody has a real choice, and this is what grabs them. It took our "A" team to add the elements that made the story work.

Toy Story 2 was great and became a critical and commercial success—and it was the defining moment for Pixar. It taught us an important lesson about the primacy of people over ideas: If you give a good idea to a mediocre team, they will screw it up; if you give a mediocre idea to a great team, they will either fix it or throw it away and come up with something that works.

Toy Story 2 also taught us another important lesson: There has to be one quality bar for every film we produce. Everyone working at the studio at the time made tremendous personal sacrifices to fix *Toy Story 2*. We shut down all the other productions. We asked our crew to work inhumane hours, and lots of people suffered repetitive stress injuries. But by rejecting mediocrity at great pain and personal sacrifice, we made a loud statement as a community that it was unacceptable to produce some good films and some mediocre films. As a result of *Toy Story 2*, it became deeply ingrained in our culture that everything we touch needs to be excellent. This goes beyond movies to the DVD production and extras, and to the toys and other consumer products associated with our characters.

Of course, most executives would at least pay lip service to the notion that they need to get good people and should set their standards high. But how many understand the importance of creating an environment that supports great people and encourages them to support one another so that the whole is far greater than the sum of the parts? That's what we are striving to do. Let me share what we've learned so far about what works.

Power to the Creatives

Creative power in a film has to reside with the film's creative leadership. As obvious as this might seem, it's not true of many companies in the movie industry and, I suspect, a lot of others. We believe the creative vision propelling each movie comes from one or two people and not from either corporate executives or a development department. Our philosophy is: You get great creative people, you bet big on them, you give them enormous leeway and support, and you provide them with an environment in which they can get honest feedback from everyone.

After *Toy Story 2* we changed the mission of our development department. Instead of coming up with new ideas for movies (its role at most studios), the department's job is to assemble small incubation teams to help directors refine their own ideas to a point where they can convince John and our other senior filmmakers that those ideas have the potential to be great films. Each team typically consists of a director, a writer, some artists, and some storyboard people. The development department's goal is to find individuals who will work effectively together. During this incubation stage, you can't judge teams by the material they're producing because it's so rough—there are many problems and open questions. But you can assess whether the teams' social dynamics are healthy and whether the teams are solving problems and making progress. Both the senior management and the development department are responsible for seeing to it that the teams function well.

To emphasize that the creative vision is what matters most, we say we are "filmmaker led." There are really two leaders: the director and the producer. They form a strong partnership. They not only strive to make a great movie but also operate within time, budget, and people constraints. (Good artists understand the value of limits.) During production, we leave the operating decisions to the film's leaders, and we don't second-guess or micromanage them.

Indeed, even when a production runs into a problem, we do everything possible to provide support without undermining their authority. One way we do this is by making it possible for a director to solicit help from our "creative brain trust" of filmmakers. (This group is a pillar of our distinctive peer-based process for making movies—an important topic I'll return to in a moment.) If this advice doesn't suffice, we'll sometimes add reinforcements to the production—such as a writer or codirector—to provide specific skills or improve the creative dynamics of the film's creative leadership.

What does it take for a director to be a successful leader in this environment? Of course, our directors have to be masters at knowing how to tell a story that will translate into the medium of film. This means that they must have a unifying vision—one that will give coherence to the thousands of ideas that go into a movie—and they must be able to turn that vision into clear directives that the staff can implement. They must set people up for success by giving them all the information they need to do the job right without telling them how to do it. Each person on a film should be given creative ownership of even the smallest task.

Good directors not only possess strong analytical skills themselves but also can harness the analytical power and life experiences of their staff members. They are superb listeners and strive to understand the thinking behind every suggestion. They appreciate all contributions, regardless of where or from whom they originate, and use the best ones.

A Peer Culture

Of great importance—and something that sets us apart from other studios—is the way people at all levels support one another. Everyone is fully invested in helping everyone else turn out the best work. They really do feel that it's all for one and one for all. Nothing exemplifies this more than our creative brain trust and our daily review process.

The brain trust

This group consists of John and our eight directors (Andrew Stanton, Brad Bird, Pete Docter, Bob Peterson, Brenda Chapman, Lee Unkrich, Gary Rydstrom, and Brad Lewis). When a director and producer feel in need of assistance, they convene the group (and anyone else they think would be valuable) and show the current version of the work in progress. This is followed by a lively two-hour give-and-take discussion, which is all about making the movie better. There's no ego. Nobody pulls any punches to be polite. This works because all the participants have come to trust and respect one another. They know it's far better to learn about problems from colleagues when there's still time to fix them than from the audience after it's too late. The problem-solving powers of this group are immense and inspirational to watch.

After a session, it's up to the director of the movie and his or her team to decide what to do with the advice; there are no mandatory notes, and the brain trust has no authority. This dynamic is crucial. It liberates the trust members so they can give their unvarnished expert opinions, and it liberates the director to seek help and fully consider the advice. It took us a while to learn this. When we tried to export the brain trust model to our technical area, we found at first that it didn't work. Eventually, I realized why: We had given these other review groups some authority. As soon as we said, "This is purely peers giving feedback to each other," the dynamic changed, and the effectiveness of the review sessions dramatically improved.

The origin of the creative brain trust was *Toy Story*. During a crisis that occurred while making that film, a special relationship developed among John, Andrew, Lee, and Joe, who had remarkable and complementary skills. Since they trusted one another, they could have very intense and heated discussions; they always knew that the passion was about the story and wasn't personal. Over time, as other people from inside and outside joined our directors' ranks, the brain trust expanded to what it is today: a community of master filmmakers who come together when needed to help one another.

The dailies

This practice of working together as peers is core to our culture, and it's not limited to our directors and producers. One example is our daily reviews, or "dailies," a process for giving and getting constant feedback in a positive way that's based on practices John observed at Disney and Industrial Light & Magic (ILM), Lucasfilm's special-effects company.

At Disney, only a small senior group would look at daily animation work. Dennis Muren, ILM's legendary visual-effects supervisor, broadened the participation to include his whole special-effects crew. (John, who joined my computer group at Lucasfilm after leaving Disney, participated in these sessions while we were creating computer-animated effects for *Young Sherlock Holmes*.)

As we built up an animation crew for *Toy Story* in the early 1990s, John used what he had learned from Disney and ILM to develop our daily review process. People show work in an incomplete state to the whole animation crew, and although the director makes decisions, everyone is encouraged to comment.

There are several benefits. First, once people get over the embarrassment of showing work still in progress, they become more creative. Second, the director or creative leads guiding the review process can communicate important points to the entire crew at the same time. Third, people learn from and inspire one another; a highly creative piece of animation will spark others to raise their game. Finally, there are no surprises at the end: When you're done, you're done. People's overwhelming desire to make sure their work is "good" before they show it to others increases the possibility that their finished version won't be what the director wants. The dailies process avoids such wasted efforts.

Technology + Art = Magic

Getting people in different disciplines to treat one another as peers is just as important as getting people within disciplines to do so. But it's much harder. Barriers include the natural class structures that arise in organizations: There always seems to be one function that considers itself and is perceived by others to be the one the organization values the most. Then there's the different languages spoken by different disciplines and even the physical distance between offices. In a creative business like ours, these barriers are impediments to producing great work, and therefore we must do everything we can to tear them down.

Walt Disney understood this. He believed that when continual change, or reinvention, is the norm in an organization and technology and art are together, magical things happen. A lot of people look back at Disney's early days and say, "Look at the artists!" They don't pay attention to his technological innovations. But he did the first sound in animation, the first color, the first compositing of animation with live action, and the first applications of xerography in animation production. He was always excited by science and technology.

At Pixar, we believe in this swirling interplay between art and technology and constantly try to use better technology at every stage of production. John coined a saying that captures this dynamic: "Technology inspires art, and art challenges the technology." To us, those aren't just words; they are a way of life that had to be established and still has to be constantly reinforced. Although we are a director- and producer-led meritocracy, which recognizes that talent is not spread equally among all people, we adhere to the following principles:

Everyone must have the freedom to communicate with anyone
This means recognizing that the decision-making hierarchy and communication structure in organizations are two different things. Members of any department should be able to approach anyone in another department to solve problems without having to go through "proper" channels. It also means that managers need to learn that they don't always have to be the first to know about something going on in their realm, and it's OK to walk into a meeting and be surprised. The impulse to tightly control the process is understandable given the complex nature of moviemaking, but problems are almost by definition unforeseen. The most efficient way to deal with numerous problems is to trust people to work out the difficulties directly with one another without having to check for permission.

It must be safe for everyone to offer ideas

We're constantly showing works in progress internally. We try to stagger who goes to which viewing to ensure that there are always fresh eyes, and everyone in the company, regardless of discipline or position, gets to go at some point. We make a concerted effort to make it safe to criticize by inviting everyone attending these showings to email notes to the creative leaders that detail what they liked and didn't like and explain why.

We must stay close to innovations happening in the academic community

We strongly encourage our technical artists to publish their research and participate in industry conferences. Publishing may give away ideas, but it keeps us connected with the academic community. This connection is worth far more than any ideas we may have revealed: It helps us attract exceptional talent and reinforces the belief throughout the company that people are more important than ideas.

We try to break down the walls between disciplines in other ways, as well. One is a collection of in-house courses we offer, which we call Pixar University. It is responsible for training and cross-training people as they develop in their careers. But it also offers an array of optional classes—many of which I've taken—that give people from different disciplines the opportunity to mix and appreciate what everyone does. Some (screenplay writing, drawing, and sculpting) are directly related to our business; some (Pilates and yoga) are not. In a sculpting class will be rank novices as well as world-class sculptors who want to refine their skills. Pixar University helps reinforce the mind-set that we're all learning and it's fun to learn together.

Our building, which is Steve Jobs's brainchild, is another way we try to get people from different departments to interact. Most buildings are designed for some functional purpose, but ours is structured to maximize inadvertent encounters. At its center is a large atrium, which contains the cafeteria, meeting rooms, bathrooms, and mailboxes. As a result, everyone has strong reasons to go there repeatedly during the course of the workday. It's hard to describe just how valuable the resulting chance encounters are.

Pixar's Operating Principles

1. Everyone must have the freedom to communicate with anyone.

2. It must be safe for everyone to offer ideas.

3. We must stay close to innovations happening in the academic community.

Staying on the Rails

Observing the rise and fall of computer companies during my career has affected me deeply. Many companies put together a phenomenal group of people who produced great products. They had the best engineers, exposure to the needs of customers, access to changing technology, and experienced management. Yet many made decisions at the height of their powers that were stunningly wrongheaded, and they faded into irrelevance. How could really smart people completely miss something so crucial to their survival? I remember asking myself more than once: "If we are ever successful, will we be equally blind?"

Many of the people I knew in those companies that failed were not very introspective. When Pixar became an independent company, I vowed we would be different. I realized that it's extremely difficult for an organization to analyze itself. It is uncomfortable and hard to be objective. Systematically fighting complacency and uncovering problems when your company is successful have got to be two of the toughest management challenges there are. Clear values, constant communication, routine postmortems, and the regular injection of outsiders who will challenge the status quo aren't enough. Strong leadership is also essential—to make sure people don't pay lip service to the values, tune out the communications, game the processes, and automatically discount newcomers' observations and suggestions. Here's a sampling of what we do:

Postmortems

The first we performed—at the end of *A Bug's Life*—was successful. But the success of those that followed varied enormously. This caused me to reflect on how to get more out of them. One thing I observed was that although people learn from the postmortems, they don't like to do them. Leaders naturally want to use the occasion to give kudos to their team members. People in general would rather talk about what went right than what went wrong. And after spending years on a film, everybody just wants to move on. Left to their own devices, people will game the system to avoid confronting the unpleasant.

There are some simple techniques for overcoming these problems. One is to try to vary the way you do the postmortems. By definition, they're supposed to be about lessons learned, so if you repeat the same format, you tend to find the same lessons, which isn't productive. Another is to ask each group to list the top five things they would do again and the top five things they wouldn't do. The balance between the positive and the negative helps make it a safer environment. In any event, employ lots of data in the review. Because we're a creative organization, people tend to assume that much of what we do can't be measured or analyzed. That's wrong. Most of our processes involve activities and deliverables that can be quantified. We keep track of the rates at which things happen, how often something has to be reworked, whether a piece of work was completely finished or not when it was sent to another department, and so on. Data can show things in a neutral way, which can stimulate discussion and challenge assumptions arising from personal impressions.

Fresh blood
Successful organizations face two challenges when bringing in new people with fresh perspectives. One is well-known—the not-invented-here syndrome. The other—the awe-of-the-institution syndrome (an issue with young new hires)—is often overlooked.

The former has not been a problem for us, thank goodness, because we have an open culture: Continually embracing change the way we do makes newcomers less threatening. Several prominent outsiders who have had a big impact on us (in terms of the exciting ideas they introduced and the strong people they attracted) were readily accepted. They include Brad Bird, who directed *The Incredibles* and *Ratatouille;* Jim Morris, who headed Industrial Light & Magic for years before joining Pixar as the producer of *WALL-E* and executive vice president of production; and Richard Hollander, a former executive of the special-effects studio Rhythm & Hues, who is leading an effort to improve our production processes.

The bigger issue for us has been getting young new hires to have the confidence to speak up. To try to remedy this, I make it a practice to speak at the orientation sessions for new hires, where I talk about the mistakes we've made and the lessons we've learned. My intent is to persuade them that we haven't gotten it all figured out and that we want everyone to question why we're doing something that doesn't seem to make sense to them. We do not want people to assume that because we are successful, everything we do is right.

For 20 years, I pursued a dream of making the first computer-animated film. To be honest, after that goal was realized—when we finished *Toy Story*—I was a bit lost. But then I realized the most exciting thing I had ever done was to help create the unique environment that allowed that film to be made. My new goal became, with John, to build a studio that had the depth, robustness, and will to keep searching for the hard truths that preserve the confluence of forces necessary to create magic. In the two years since Pixar's merger with Disney, we've had the good fortune to expand that goal to include the revival of Disney Animation Studios. It has been extremely gratifying to see the principles and approaches we developed at Pixar transform this studio. But the ultimate test of whether John and I have achieved our goals is if Pixar and Disney are still producing animated films that touch world culture in a positive way long after we two, and our friends who founded and built Pixar with us, are gone.

Originally published in September 2008. Reprint R0809D

49

Putting Your Company's Whole Brain to Work

by Dorothy Leonard and Susaan Straus

Note: Details on specific personality assessment instruments have been removed from the article because those instruments have changed since the article was first published.

INNOVATE OR FALL BEHIND: The competitive imperative for virtually all businesses today is that simple. Achieving it is hard, however, because innovation takes place when different ideas, perceptions, and ways of processing and judging information collide. That, in turn, often requires collaboration among various players who see the world in inherently different ways. As a result, the conflict that should take place constructively among ideas all too often ends up taking place unproductively among people who do not innately understand one another. Disputes become personal, and the creative process breaks down.

Generally, managers have two responses to this phenomenon. On the one hand, managers who dislike conflict—or value only their own approach—actively avoid the clash of ideas. They hire and reward people of a particular stripe, usually people like themselves. Their organizations fall victim to what we call the *comfortable clone syndrome:* Coworkers share similar interests and training; everyone thinks alike. Because all ideas pass through similar cognitive screens, only familiar ones survive. For example, a new-business development group formed entirely of employees with the same disciplinary background and set of experiences will assess every idea with an unvarying set of assumptions and analytical tools. Such a group will struggle to innovate, often in vain.

On the other hand, managers who value employees with a variety of thinking styles frequently don't understand how to manage them. They act as if locking a group of diverse individuals in the same room will necessarily result in a creative solution to a problem. They overlook the fact that people with different styles often don't understand or respect one another, and that such differences can fuel personal disagreements. The "detail guy" dismisses the "vision thing"; the "concept man" deplores endless analysis; and the individualist considers the demands of a team an utter waste of time. They simply can't work together without help.

The manager successful at fostering innovation figures out how to get different approaches to grate against one another in a productive process we call *creative abrasion*. Such a manager understands that different people have different thinking styles: analytical or intuitive, conceptual or experiential, social or independent, logical or values driven. She deliberately designs a full spectrum of approaches and perspectives into her organization—whether that organization is a team, a work group, or an entire company—and she understands that cognitively diverse people must respect the thinking styles of others. She sets ground rules for working together to discipline the creative process. Above all, the manager who wants to encourage innovation in her organization needs to examine what she does to promote or inhibit creative abrasion.

We have worked with a number of organizations over the years and have observed many managers who know how to make creative abrasion work for them. In order to create new ideas and products, such managers actively manage the process of bringing together a variety of people who think and act in potentially conflicting ways.

Idea in Brief

Successful innovation relies on people—and people have different cognitive approaches for assimilating data and solving problems:

- So-called "left-brain" thinkers tend to approach a problem in a logical, analytical way. "Right-brain" thinkers rely more on nonlinear, intuitive approaches.

- Some people prefer to work together to solve a problem; others like to gather and process information by themselves.

- Abstract thinkers need to learn about something before they experience it; for experiential people, it's just the opposite.

Cognitive differences are often subtle; people don't naturally appreciate their significance. Managers who dislike conflict or who value only their own approach often fall victim to the **comfortable clone syndrome**, surrounding themselves with people who think alike and who share similar interests and training. Even managers who value intellectual diversity may not realize how difficult it can be for people with different styles to understand or respect one another. But to achieve **creative abrasion**, you have to make the different approaches rub together in productive ways.

How We Think

What we call *cognitive differences* are varying approaches to perceiving and assimilating data, making decisions, solving problems, and relating to other people. These approaches are *preferences* (not to be confused with skills or abilities). For instance, you may prefer to approach problems intuitively but in fact may be better trained to approach them analytically. Preferences are not rigid: Most people can draw on a mixture of approaches and do not live their lives within narrow cognitive boundaries. We often stretch outside the borders of our preferred operating modes if the conditions are right and the stakes are high enough. That said, we all tend to have one or two preferred habits of thought that influence our decision-making styles and our interactions with others—for good or for ill.

The most widely recognized cognitive distinction is between left-brained and right-brained ways of thinking. This

Idea in Practice

To get creative abrasion, start by compiling a cognitive profile of your team. Engage a trained professional to administer one of several readily available diagnostic tools.

1. **Do your own profile first.** Become familiar with the ways in which your preferences shape your leadership and patterns of communication. If you're not paying attention, your own style can stifle the very creativity you're looking to foster among team members.

2. **Create "whole-brained" teams.** Once you understand your own thinking styles and those of the other team members, identify the styles that are missing so that you'll

know what to focus on when hiring opportunities arise. This results in a team with a wider variety of problem-solving approaches. At Nissan Design, Jerry Hirschberg hires designers in pairs—a free-form thinker alongside someone with a more analytical approach—to ensure intellectual diversity. If you don't have the luxury of hiring new people, look elsewhere in the company for the critical thinking styles your group lacks.

3. **Employ strategies that exploit the team's full spectrum of approaches.** At Xerox PARC, anthropologists work alongside computer scientists to create cyberspace meeting rooms

categorization is more powerful metaphorically than it is accurate physiologically; not all the functions commonly associated with the left brain are located on the left side of the cortex, and not all so-called right-brained functions are located on the right. Still, the simple description does usefully capture radically different ways of thinking. An analytical, logical, and sequential approach to problem framing and solving (left-brained thinking) clearly differs from an intuitive, values-based, and nonlinear one (right-brained thinking).

Cognitive preferences also reveal themselves in work styles and decision-making activities. Take collaboration as opposed to independence. Some people prefer to work together on solving problems, whereas others prefer to gather, absorb, and process information by themselves. Each type does its best work under different conditions. Or consider thinking as opposed to feeling. Some people evaluate that have a welcoming, human touch in addition to being technologically sophisticated.

4. **Actively manage the creative process.** Abrasion is not creative unless managers make it so.

- Take time at the outset to acknowledge team members' differences.

- Before problems surface, devise clear, simple guidelines for working together. For example, one group decided to handle conflict by stating that anyone could disagree with anyone else about anything, but no one could disagree without saying the reason.

- Keep the project's goal in front of the group at all times.

- When scheduling a project, create time for both divergent thinking (uncovering imaginative alternatives) and convergent thinking (focusing in on one option and then implementing it).

- Don't treat team members the way you want to be treated—tailor your communications to the receiver.

- Depersonalize conflict when it does arise. Acknowledge that other approaches are not wrongheaded, just different.

evidence and make decisions through a structured, logical process, whereas others rely on their values and emotions to guide them to the appropriate action.

The list goes on. Abstract thinkers, for instance, assimilate information from a variety of sources, such as books, reports, videos, and conversations. They prefer learning *about* something rather than experiencing it directly. Experiential people, in contrast, get information from interacting directly with people and things. Some people demand quick decisions no matter the issue, whereas others prefer to generate a lot of options no matter the urgency. One type focuses on details, whereas the other looks for the big picture: the relationships and patterns that the data forms.

Not surprisingly, people tend to choose professions that reward their own combination of preferences. Their work experience, in turn, reinforces the original preferences and deepens the associated skills. Therefore, one sees very different problem-solving approaches among accountants, entrepreneurs, social workers, and artists. Proof to an engineer, for example, resides in the numbers. But show a page of numerical data to a playwright, and, more persuaded by his intuition, he may well toss it aside. Of course, assessing people's likely approaches to problem solving only by their discipline can be as misleading as using gender or ethnicity as a guide. Within any profession, there are always people whose thinking styles are at odds with the dominant approach.

The best way for managers to assess the thinking styles of the people they are responsible for is to use an established diagnostic instrument as an assessment tool. A well-tested tool is both more objective and more thorough than the impressions of even the most sensitive and observant of managers. Dozens of diagnostic tools and descriptive analyses of human personality have been developed to identify categories of cognitive approaches to problem solving and communication. All the instruments agree on the following basic points:

- Preferences are neither inherently good nor inherently bad. They are assets or liabilities depending on the situation. For example, politicians or CEOs who prefer to think out loud in public create expectations that they sometimes cannot meet, but the person who requires quiet reflection before acting can be a liability in a crisis.

- Distinguishing preferences emerge early in our lives, and strongly held ones tend to remain relatively stable through the years. Thus, for example, those of us who crave certainty are unlikely ever to have an equal love of ambiguity and paradox.

- We can learn to expand our repertoire of behaviors, to act outside our preferred styles. But that is difficult—like writing with the opposite hand.

- Understanding others' preferences helps people communicate and collaborate.

Managers who use credible personality instruments find that their employees accept the outcomes of the tests and use them to improve their processes and behaviors.

How We Act

All the assessment in the world means nothing unless new understanding brings different actions. Personality analysis instruments will help you understand yourself and will help others understand themselves. The managerial challenge is to use the insights that these instruments offer to create new processes and encourage new behaviors that will help innovation efforts succeed.

Understand yourself

Start with yourself. When you identify your own style, you gain insight into the ways your preferences unconsciously shape your style of leadership and patterns of communication. You may be surprised to discover that your style can stifle the very creativity you seek from your employees. Consider the experiences of two managers of highly creative organizations. Each was at odds with his direct reports—but for very different reasons.

Jim Shaw, executive vice president of MTV Networks, is a left-brained guy in a right-brained organization. Said Shaw:

I have always characterized the creative, right-brained, visionary-type people here as dreamers. What I've realized is that when a dreamer expressed a vision, my gut reaction was to say, 'Well, if you want to do that, what you've got to do is A, then B, then you have to work out C, and because you've got no people and you've got no satellite uplink, you'll have to do D and E.' I've learned that saying that to a creative type is like throwing up on the dream. When I say that stuff too soon, the dreamer personalizes it as an attack. I've learned not to put all of the things that need to be done on the table initially. I can't just blurt it all out—it makes me look like a naysayer. What I've learned to do is to leak the information gradually, then the dreamer knows that I am meeting him halfway.

Jerry Hirshberg, president of Nissan Design International, ran into precisely the opposite problem. Hirshberg discovered that some of his employees craved the very kind of structure that he personally abhorred. Before this epiphany, he inundated them with information and expected creativity in return. In short, he tried to manage his employees the way *he* would have wanted to be managed. Hirshberg found, however, that a few individuals reacted to every suggestion with a "yes, but . . ." Initially, he interpreted such hesitancy as an anti-innovation bias. But he eventually realized that some of his employees preferred to have more time both to digest problems and to construct logical approaches to his intuitively derived ideas. Given a bit of extra time, they would return to the project with solid, helpful, and insightful plans for implementation. Ironically, it was their commitment to the success of the initiative that caused the employees to hesitate: They wanted the best possible result. Hirshberg recognized that their contributions were as critical as his own or those of any of the other "right-brainers" in the company.

Both Shaw and Hirshberg came to realize that their own cognitive preferences unconsciously shaped their leadership styles and communication patterns. In fact, their automatic reactions initially stifled the very creativity they sought from their employees. And note that it was just as important for the predominantly right-brained manager to recognize the contributions of the logicians as it was for the left-brained manager to acknowledge the organic approach of the visionaries. Except in theoretical models, creativity is not the exclusive province of one side or the other.

If you want an innovative organization, you need to hire, work with, and promote people who make you uncomfortable. You need to understand your own preferences so that you can complement your weaknesses and exploit your strengths. The biggest barrier to recognizing the contributions of people who are unlike you is your own ego. Suppose you are stalled on a difficult problem. To whom do you go for help? Usually to someone who is on the same wavelength or to someone whose opinion you respect. These people may give you soothing strokes, but they are unlikely to help spark a new idea. Suppose you were to take the problem instead to someone with whom you often find yourself at odds, someone who rarely validates your ideas or perspectives. It may take courage and tact to get constructive feedback, and the process may not be exactly pleasant. But that feedback will likely improve the quality of your solution. And when your adversary recovers from his amazement at your request, he may even get along with you better because the disagreement was clearly intellectual, not personal.

Forget the golden rule
Don't treat people the way you want to be treated. Tailor communications to the receiver instead of the sender. In a cognitively diverse environment, a message sent is not necessarily a message received. Some people respond well to facts, figures, and statistics. Others prefer anecdotes. Still others digest graphic presentations most easily. Information must be delivered in the preferred "language" of the recipient if it is to be received at all.

For example, say you want to persuade an organization to adopt an open office layout. Arguments appealing to the analytical mind would rely on statistics from well-documented research conducted by objective experts that prove that open architecture enhances the effectiveness of communication. Arguments geared toward the action-oriented type would answer specific questions about implementation: How long will the office conversion take? Exactly what kind of furniture is needed? What are the implications for acoustics? Arguments aimed at people-oriented individuals would focus on such questions as, How does an open office affect relationships? How would this setup affect morale? and Are people happy in this sort of setup? Arguments crafted for people with a future-oriented perspective would include graphics as well as artists' renderings of the proposed environment. In short, regardless of how you personally would prefer to deliver the message, you will be more persuasive and better understood if you formulate messages to appeal to the particular thinking style of your listener.

Create "whole-brained" teams

Either over time or by initial design, company or group cultures can become dominated by one particular cognitive style. IBM, in the days when it was known as "Big Blue," presented a uniform face to the world; Digital Equipment prided itself on its engineering culture. Such homogeneity makes for efficient functioning—and limited approaches to problems or opportunities. Companies with strong cultures can indeed be very creative, but within predictable boundaries: say, clever marketing or imaginative engineering. When the market demands that such companies innovate in different ways, they have to learn new responses. Doing so requires adopting a variety of approaches to solving a problem—using not just the right brain or the left brain but the *whole* brain.

Consider the all-too-common error made by John, a rising star in a large, diversified instrument company: He forfeited an important career opportunity because he failed to see the need for a whole-brained team. Appointed manager of a new-product development group, John had a charter to bring in radically innovative ideas for products and services for launch in three to six years. "Surprise me," the CEO said.

Given a free hand in hiring, John lured in three of the brightest MBAs he could find. They immediately went to work conducting industry analyses and sorting through existing product possibilities, applying their recently acquired skills in financial analysis. To complete the team, John turned to the pile of résumés on his desk sent to him by human resources. All the applicants had especially strong quantitative skills, and a couple were engineers. John was pleased. Surely a group of such intelligent, well-trained, rigorous thinkers would be able to come up with some radical innovations for the company. Ignoring advice to hire some right-brained people to stimulate different ideas, he continued to populate his group with left-brained wizards. After 18 months, the team had rejected all the proposed new projects in the pipeline on the basis of well-argued and impressively documented financial and technical risk analysis. But the team's members had not come up with a single new idea. The CEO was neither surprised nor pleased, and the group was disbanded just short of its second anniversary.

In contrast, Bob, a successful entrepreneur embarking on his latest venture, resisted the strong temptation to tolerate only like-minded people. He knew from his prior ventures that his highly analytical style alienated some of his most creative people. Despite his unusual degree of self-awareness, Bob came within a hair's breadth of firing a strong and experienced manager: Wally, his director of human resources. According to Bob, after several months on board, Wally appeared to be "a quart and a half low." Why? Because he was inattentive in budget meetings and focused on what Bob perceived as trivia—day care, flextime, and benefits. Before taking action, however, Bob decided to look at the management team through the lens of thinking styles. He soon realized that Wally was exactly the kind of person he needed to help him grow his small company. Wally contributed a key element that was otherwise missing in the management team: a sensitivity to human needs that helped the company foresee and forestall problems with employees. So Bob learned to meet Wally halfway. Describing his success in learning to work with Wally, he told us, "You would have been proud of me. I started our meetings with five minutes of dogs, kids, and station wagons." Although the concern Wally demonstrated for the workers in the company did not eliminate union issues completely, it did minimize antagonism toward management and made disputes easier to resolve.

The list of whole-brained teams that continue to innovate successfully is long. At Xerox PARC, social scientists work alongside computer scientists. For instance, computer scientist Pavel Curtis, who is creating a virtual world in which people will meet and mingle, is working with an anthropologist who understands how communities form. As a result, Curtis's cyberspace meeting places have more human touches and are more welcoming than they would have been had they been designed only by scientists. Another example is the PARC PAIR (PARC Artist In Residence) program, which links computer scientists with artists so that each may influence the other's perceptions and representations of the world.

At Interval Research, a California think tank dedicated to multimedia technologies, Director David Liddle invites leaders from various disciplines to visit for short "sabbaticals." The purpose is to stimulate a cross-fertilization of ideas and approaches to solving problems. The resulting exchanges have helped Interval Research create and spin off several highly innovative start-ups. And Jerry Hirshberg applies the whole-brain principle to hiring practices at Nissan Design by bringing designers into his organization in virtual pairs. That is, when he hires a designer who glories in the freedom of pure color and rhythm, he will next hire a very rational, Bauhaus-trained designer who favors analysis and focuses on function.

Complete homogeneity in an organization's cognitive approach can be very efficient. But as managers at Xerox PARC, Interval Research, and Nissan Design have learned, no matter how brilliant the group of individuals, their contributions to innovative problem solving are enhanced by coming up against totally different perspectives.

Look for the ugly duckling

Suppose you don't have the luxury of hiring new people yet find your organization mired in a swamp of stale thinking patterns. Consider the experience of the CEO of the U.S. subsidiary of a tightly controlled and conservative European chemical company. Even though the company's business strategy had never worked well in the United States, headquarters pushed the CEO to do more of the same. He knew he needed to figure out a fresh approach because the U.S. company was struggling to compete in a rapidly changing marketplace. But his direct reports were as uniformly left-brained as his superiors in Europe and were disinclined to work with him to figure out new solutions.

Rather than give up, the CEO tested thinking preferences further down in the organization. He found the cognitive disparity that he needed in managers one layer below his direct reports—a small but dynamic set of individuals whose countercultural thinking patterns had constrained their advancement. In this company, people with right-brained preferences were seen as helpful but were not considered top management material. They were never promoted above a certain level.

The CEO changed that. He elevated three managers with right-brained proclivities to the roles of senior vice president and division head—lofty positions occupied until then exclusively by left-brained individuals. The new executives were strong supporters of the CEO's intentions to innovate and worked with him to develop new approaches to the business. They understood that their communication strategy with headquarters would be critical to their success. They deliberately packaged their new ideas in a way that appealed to the cognitive framework of their European owner. Instead of lecturing about the need to change and try new ideas as they had in the past, the Americans presented their ideas as ways of solving problems. They supported their positions with well-researched quantitative data and with calculated anticipated cost savings and ROI—and described how similar approaches had succeeded elsewhere. They detailed the specific steps they would follow to succeed. Within two years, the U.S. subsidiary embarked on a major organizational redesign effort that included such radical notions as permitting outside competition for internal services. The quality of internal services soared—as did the number of innovations generated by the company in the United States.

Manage the creative process

Abrasion is not creative unless managers make it so. Members of whole-brained teams don't naturally understand one another, and they can easily come to dislike one another. Successful managers of richly diverse groups spend time from the outset getting members to acknowledge their differences—often through a joint exploration of the results of a diagnostic analysis—and devise guidelines for working together before attempting to act on the problem at hand. Managers who find it awkward or difficult to lead their groups in identifying cognitive styles or in establishing guidelines can usually enlist the aid of someone who is trained in facilitation.

People often feel a bit foolish creating rules about how they will work together. Surely, the thinking goes, we are all adults and have years of experience in dealing with group dynamics. That, of course, is the problem. Everyone has practiced dysfunctional behavior for years. We learn to value politeness over truth at our mothers' knees. (Who hasn't mastered the art of the white lie by age 16?) We often discount an argument if it has an element of emotion or passion. We opt out if we feel ignored—people with unappreciated thinking styles learn to sit against the wall during meetings (the organizational "back of the bus"). And we usually don't even notice those behaviors because they are so routine.

But the cost of allowing such behaviors to overtake a group is too high. Bob Meyers, senior vice president of interactive media at NBC, uses a sports analogy to make the point: "On a football team, for example, you have to use all kinds of people. Like the little, skinny guy who can only kick the ball. He may not even look as if he belongs on the team. This guy can't stand up to the refrigerator types that play in other positions. But as long as he does his job, he doesn't need to be big. He can just do what he does best. The catch is that the team needs to recognize what the little skinny guy can do—or they lose the benefit of his talent."

Managing the process of creative abrasion means making sure that everyone is at the front of the bus and talking. Some simple but powerful techniques can be helpful. First, clarify why you are working together by keeping the common goal in front of the group at all times. "If the goal is a real-world one with shared accountability and timetables attached," one manager observed, "then everyone understands the relevance of honoring one another's differences."

Second, make your operating guidelines explicit. Effective guidelines are always simple, clear, and concise. For example, one group set up the following principles about handling disagreements: "Anyone can disagree about anything with anyone, but no one can disagree without stating the reason" and "When someone states an objection, everyone else should listen to it, try to understand it, treat it as legitimate, and counter with their reasons if they don't agree with it." Some principles are as simple as "discuss taboo subjects," "verify assumptions," and "arrive on time with your homework done."

Third, set up an agenda ahead of time that explicitly provides enough time for both *divergent* discussion to uncover imaginative alternatives and *convergent* discussion to select an option and plan its implementation. Innovation requires both types of discussion, but people who excel at different types can, as one manager observed, "drive each other nuts." Another manager said, "If you ask people comfortable with ambiguity whether they prefer A or B, they will ask, 'How about C?'" Meanwhile, the people who crave closure will be squirming in their seats at the seemingly pointless discussion. Moreover, if one approach dominates, the unbalanced group process can risk producing an unacceptable or unfeasible new product, service, or change. Clearly allocating time to the two different types of discussion will contain the frustrations of both the decisive types, who are constantly looking at their watches wanting the decision to be made now, and the ambiguous types, who want to be sure that all possible avenues for creativity have been explored. Otherwise, the decisive members generally will pound the others into silence by invoking time pressures and scheduling. They will grab the first viable option rather than the best one. Or if the less decisive dominate, the group may never reach a conclusion. Innovation requires both divergent and convergent thinking, both brainstorming and action plans.

Depersonalize conflict

Diverse cognitive preferences can cause tremendous tensions in any group, yet innovation requires the cross-fertilization of ideas. And because many new products are systems rather than stand-alone pieces, many business projects cannot proceed without the cooperation of people who receive different messages from the same words and make different observations about the same incidents. The single most valuable contribution that understanding different thinking and communication styles brings to the process of innovation is taking the sting out of intellectual disagreements that turn personal.

Consider the experience of the product manager of a radically new product for a medical supplies company. Facing a strict deadline of just 14 months to design and deliver a new surgical instrument, the manager's team needed to pull together fast. Design felt misled by marketing, however, and manufacturing couldn't understand design's delay in choosing between two mechanical hinges. The disagreements turned personal, starting with "you always . . ." and ending with "irresponsible ignorance." Two months into the project, the manager began to wonder whether he should disband the team and start over again. But he knew that his boss, the vice president of marketing, would not agree to extend the deadline. "I was desperate," he recalled. "I decided to make one last attempt at getting them to work together."

The manager decided to experiment with an off-site gathering of his staff, including sessions diagnosing cognitive preferences. When they returned to work, the team members used the new language they had learned to label their differences in opinion and style. "At first, using the terms was kind of a joke," the manager recalled. "They'd say things like, 'Well, of course I want the schedule right now. I'm a J!' Yet you could tell that people were really seeing one another in a different light, and they weren't getting angry." The team made its deadline; perhaps even more important, several members voluntarily joined forces to work on the next iteration of the product. This willingness to work together generated more value for the company than just "warm fuzzies." Critical technical knowledge was preserved in one small, colocated group—knowledge that would have been scattered had project members dispersed to different product lines. Moreover, keeping part of the team together resulted in a rapid development time for the derivative product.

People who do not understand cognitive preferences tend to personalize conflict or avoid it—or both. The realization that another person's approach is not wrongheaded and stubborn, but merely predictably different, diffuses anger. For example, at Viacom, a planning session involving two managers had ground to a halt. One manager simply wouldn't buy in to the idea that the other was presenting. Suddenly, the presenter slapped his head and said, "Oooohhh! I get it! You're left-brained! Give me half an hour to switch gears, and I'll be right back. Let me try this one more time." The left-brained manager laughingly agreed—he understood the paradigm—and the meeting resumed with the presenter armed with quantitative data and a much more cohesive and logical presentation. Establishing that kind of effective two-way communication led to a common understanding of the issues at hand and, ultimately, a solution.

Understanding that someone views a problem differently does not mean you will agree. But an important element in understanding thinking styles is recognizing that no one style is inherently better than another. Each style brings a uniquely valuable perspective to the process of innovation, just as each style has some negatives associated with it. Stereotypes of the coldhearted logician; the absent-minded, creative scientist; and the bleeding-heart liberal have some basis in reality. If people even partially internalize the inherent value of different perspectives, they will take disagreements less personally and will be better able to argue and reach a compromise or a consensus with less animosity. They will be open to the possibility that an alien view of the world might actually enhance their own. They will be better equipped to listen for the "aha" that occurs at the intersection of different planes of thought.

Caveat Emptor

Personality analysis of the type we describe is no more than a helpful tool, and it has many limitations. The diagnostic instruments measure only one aspect of personality: preferences in thinking styles and communication. They do not measure ability or intelligence, and they do not predict performance. It is difficult to measure other qualities that are critical to successful innovation such as courage, curiousity, integrity, empathy, and drive.

Preferences tend to be relatively stable, but life experiences can affect them. For example, repeated application of one instrument over a period of years has revealed a tendency for people to drift from a thinking style toward a feeling style when they have children. For the most part, however, studies suggest that people retain their dominant preferences throughout a variety of work and social circumstances.

One critical warning label should be attached to any of these diagnostic instruments: Only trained individuals should administer them. Not only can results be incorrectly interpreted (for instance, what are intended to be neutral descriptions of preferences might be labeled "right" or "wrong" behavior), but they can also be misused to invade people's privacy or to stereotype them. Of course, it is a human tendency to simplify in order to comprehend complexities; we stereotype people all the time on the basis of their language, dress, and behavior. Because these diagnostics have the weight of considerable psychological research behind them, however, they can be dangerous when misused. Without structured, reliable diagnoses, judgments are likely to be superficial and flawed. And without a substantial investment of time and resources, managers can't expect abrasion to be creative.

One of the paradoxes of modern management is that, in the midst of technical and social change so pervasive and rapid that it seems out of pace with the rhythms of nature, human personality has not altered throughout recorded history. People have always had distinct preferences in their approaches to problem solving. Why then is it only now becoming so necessary for managers to understand those differences? Because today's complex products demand integrating the expertise of individuals who do not innately understand one another. Today's pace of change demands that these individuals quickly develop the ability to work together. If abrasion is not managed into creativity, it will constrict the constructive impulses of individuals and organizations alike. Rightly harnessed, the energy released by the intersection of different thought processes will propel innovation.

Originally published in July–August 1997. Reprint 97407

Find Innovation Where You Least Expect It

by Tony McCaffrey and Jim Pearson

ON THE EVENING of April 14, 1912, the RMS *Titanic* collided with an iceberg in the North Atlantic and sunk two hours and 40 minutes later. Of its 2,200 passengers and crew, only 705 survived, plucked out of 16 lifeboats by the *Carpathia*. Imagine how many more might have lived if crew members had thought of the iceberg as not just the cause of the disaster but a lifesaving solution. The iceberg rose high above the water and stretched some 400 feet in length. The lifeboats might have ferried people there to look for a flat spot. The *Titanic* itself was navigable for a while and might have been able to pull close enough to the iceberg for people to scramble on. Such a rescue operation was not without precedent: Some 60 years before, 127 of 176 passengers emigrating from Ireland to Canada saved themselves in the Gulf of St. Lawrence by climbing aboard an ice floe.

It's impossible to know if this rescue attempt would have worked. At the least it's an intriguing idea—yet surprisingly difficult to envision. If you were to ask a group of executives, even creative product managers and marketers, to come up with innovative scenarios in which all the *Titanic*'s passengers could have been saved, they would very likely have the same blind spot as the crew. The reason is a common psychological bias—called *functional fixedness*—that limits a person to seeing an object only in the way in which it is traditionally used. In a nautical context, an iceberg is a hazard to be avoided; it's very hard to see it any other way.

When it comes to innovation, businesses are constantly hampered by functional fixedness and other cognitive biases that cause people to overlook elegant solutions hidden in plain sight. We have spent years investigating how innovative designs can be built by harnessing the power of the commonly overlooked. We have identified techniques and tools to help overcome cognitive traps and solve problems in innovative ways—whether conceiving new products, finding novel applications for existing products, or anticipating competitive threats. Using the tools doesn't require special talents or heroic degrees of creativity; taken together, they form a simple, low-cost, systematic way to spur innovation.

To understand how the tools work, let's first look at the three cognitive barriers they address.

Functional Fixedness

In the 1930s, the German psychologist Karl Duncker demonstrated the phenomenon of functional fixedness with a famous brainteaser. He gave subjects a candle, a box of thumbtacks, and a book of matches and asked them to find a way to affix the candle to the wall so that when it was lit, wax would not drip onto the floor. Many people had a hard time realizing that the answer was to empty the box of tacks, attach the candle to the inside of the box with melted wax, and then tack the box to the wall. The box acts as a shelf that supports the candle and catches the dripping wax. Because the box had been presented to subjects as a tack holder, they couldn't see it any other way.

In similar puzzles—known by cognitive psychologists as "insight problems"—people have trouble seeing that in a pinch a plastic lawn chair could be used as a paddle (turn it over, grab two legs, and start rowing); that a basketball could be deflated, formed into the shape of a bowl, and used to safely carry hot coals from one campsite to another; or that a candlewick could be used to tie things together (scrape the wax away to free the string).

What causes functional fixedness? When we see a common object, we automatically screen out awareness of features that are

Idea in Brief

Context

The tendency to fixate on the most common use of an object—a bias researchers call "functional fixedness"—is a serious barrier to innovation. The problem is that we see the object's use rather than the object itself.

Key Idea

We can overcome this bias—and similar biases about the object's design and purpose—by changing how we describe the object and how we think about its component parts.

In Practice

An alternative to brainstorming, which the authors call *brainswarming*, brings these techniques to life.

Overcoming functional fixedness

Breaking an object down into its component parts can reveal new uses.

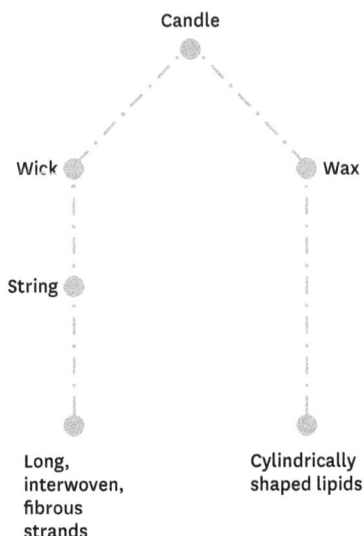

Candle

Wick   Wax

String

Long, interwoven, fibrous strands   Cylindrically shaped lipids

---

not important for its use. This is an efficient neurological tactic for everyday life, but it's the enemy of innovation.

One way to overcome the problem is to change how you describe an object. When told that a candlewick is a string, for instance, almost everyone recognizes that it could be used to tie things together. Our "generic parts technique" is a systematic way to change the way an object is described to avoid unintentionally narrowing people's conception of it, opening them to more ideas for its uses.

We consider each element of an object in turn and ask two questions: "Can it be broken down further?" and "Does our description imply a particular use?" If the answer to either question is yes, we keep breaking down the elements until they're described in their most general terms, mapping the results on a simple tree. When an iceberg is described generically as a floating surface 200 feet to 400 feet long, its potential as a lifesaving platform soon emerges. (See the exhibit "Overcoming functional fixedness" for a visualization of the parts of a candle.)

Calling something a "wick" implies its use as a conduit of a flame. Describing it as a "string" strips away a layer of preconceived uses and suggests less common ones. Breaking the string down further into its constituent parts of "fibrous strands" might spark even more uses.

To see if generating generic descriptions bolsters creative thinking, our research team presented two groups of students with eight insight problems that required overcoming the functional fixedness bias in order to solve. We told the members of one group simply to try their best. We taught the other group the generic parts technique and then asked them to use it on the problems. The people in the first group were able to solve, on average, 49% of the problems (just shy of four of them). Those who systematically engaged in creating generic descriptions of their resources were able to solve, on average, 83% (or 6.64) of them.

Design Fixation

Simple insight problems given in a psychology lab can be solved by focusing on only four types of features—materials, size, shape, and parts. But solutions to real-world engineering problems often

Promising features for a pouch

If you consider an object's less obvious characteristics, new purposes may arise. Some features to consider in the case of a candy pouch are:

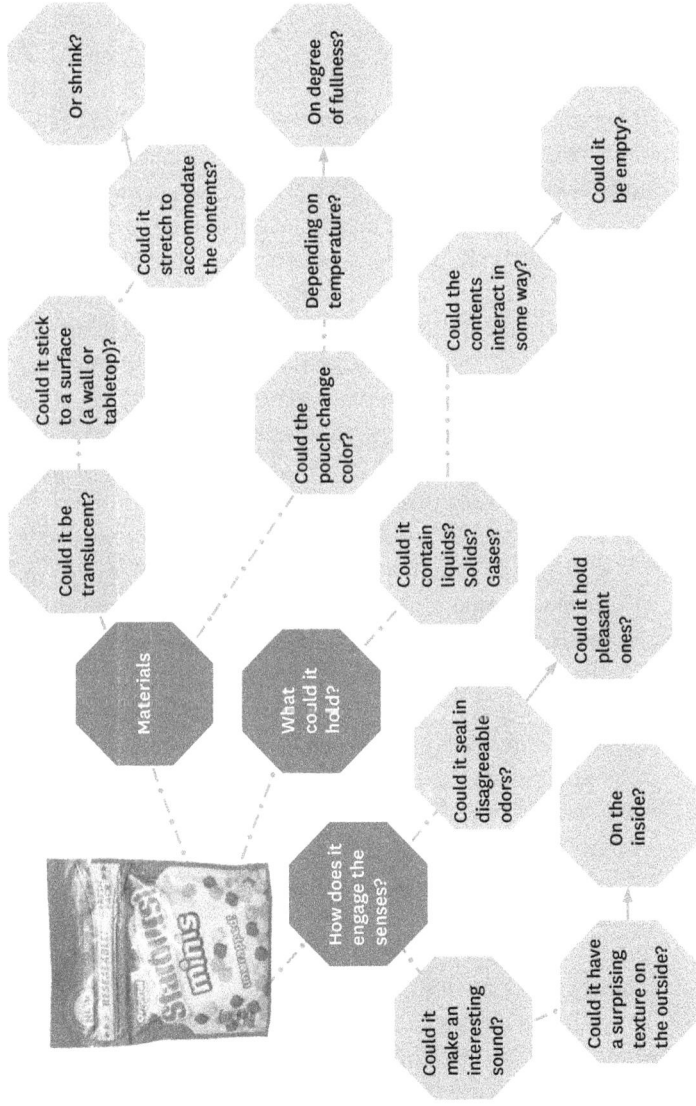

- Or shrink?
- Could it stretch to accommodate the contents?
- Could it stick to a surface (a wall or tabletop)?
- Could it be translucent?
- **Materials**

- On degree of fullness?
- Depending on temperature?
- Could the pouch change color?

- **What could it hold?**
- Could it contain liquids? Solids? Gases?
- Could the contents interact in some way?
- Could it be empty?

- **How does it engage the senses?**
- Could it seal in disagreeable odors?
- Could it hold pleasant ones?
- Could it make an interesting sound?
- Could it have a surprising texture on the outside?
- On the inside?

depend on noticing unusual aspects of a broader range of features. This, as we noted, is very difficult to do.

We studied this phenomenon by asking 15 people to list as many features and associations as they could for a candle, a broom, and a dozen other common objects. We then classified their responses by the type of feature, including its color, shape, material, designed use, and aesthetic properties, along with the emotions it evokes, the type of energy it generates, and the objects it's commonly paired with. On average, participants overlooked almost 21 of the 32 types of features (about 65%) that we had previously identified for each object.

Why? When handed a product and asked to create a new design or variation on it, people tend to fixate on the features of the current design. This obstacle to novelty is called design fixation. To take a real-world example, when people are shown a sturdy, resealable pouch full of candy and asked to think of a new design that could lead to new uses, they tend to manipulate the types of features used to create the current design—that is, they focus on the width of the base of the pouch or the rigidity of the plastic that makes it stand. To be truly innovative, however, you need to manipulate the features that everyone else has overlooked.

But how do you do that? Just as airline pilots have long used checklists to make sure they don't skip any necessary steps when preparing for flight, we developed a checklist of types of product features that people tend to overlook. Whether your product is a physical object or an intangible process, we recommend that you develop a checklist of features that were important to your previous and current innovation projects and add to the list with each new project. Teams working on innovation projects can then refer to the list to prompt them to consider features they would probably overlook—thus saving time, effort, and frustration. Examining the pouch of candy with our checklist in mind permitted us to easily uncover many features that could lead to new designs and new uses. First, every pouch sold has something in it. This feature is so obvious that its absence is commonly overlooked. Why not sell empty pouches so that customers can decide what to use them for: jewelry, spare change, nuts and bolts, cosmetics, and so on? Imagine empty pouches next to the sandwich bags, freezer bags, and storage bags in your supermarket. Second, most pouches sold are about the size of your hand. Systematically considering changes to the size triggers new ideas for possible contents. What about selling a gallon of paint in a resealable pouch, for instance? Third, current pouches have one inner compartment. But what might you do with more? You could, say, sell two-compartment pouches for things you want to mix together later: cereal in the top compartment and milk in the bottom, salad in the bottom and dressing in the top, and so on. Fourth, consider the pouch as a container of aroma (or as a guard against it). You could sell a large pouch as a garbage can that reseals to keep in the odor. These are just a few of the new designs that emerge from contemplating a checklist of overlooked features.

Goal Fixedness

Suppose we asked you to think of a way to adhere something to a garbage can. Chances are that like most people, you would think of using glue or tape, both forms of adhesives. But what if we asked you instead to *fasten* something to the can? Just switching a specific verb like "adhere" to a more general one would most likely prompt you to list a wider range of possibilities: binder clip, paper clip, nail, string, Velcro, and so on. That's because the way a goal is phrased often

What's in a name?

How broadly—or narrowly—you phrase a goal affects how you visualize it.

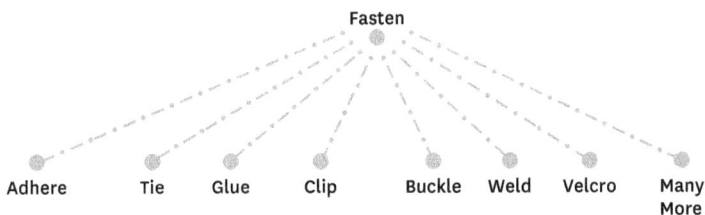

Fasten
Adhere · Tie · Glue · Clip · Buckle · Weld · Velcro · Many More

narrows people's thinking. We call this barrier "goal fixedness." Framing a problem in more general terms can help overcome it.

But it can be hard to determine what constitutes a "more general term." Is "fasten" more general than "adhere"? A good resource for mapping terms is a thesaurus that makes hierarchical structure explicit by identifying hyponyms—more-specific synonyms—for them. For example, the online thesaurus WordNet indicates that there are least 61 ways to fasten things—including sew, clamp, chain, garter, strap, hook, staple, belt, screw, wire, buckle, cement, tack, joggle, button, and rivet. Each describes the concept of fastening one thing to another in a slightly different way and gives rise to diverse solutions. "Adhere," by contrast, has only four hyponyms.

Action words, the centerpiece of most goals, often have hyponyms. Each hyponym hints at a more specific way to achieve the goal. There are 172 for the verb "remove," 50 for "guide," 46 for "transport," 115 terms for "separate," and—perhaps surprisingly— only 24 for the seemingly very general term "mix."

Of course, a goal consists of more than just a verb. The verb expresses what sort of change you're after, but nouns express what needs changing, and prepositional phrases express important constraints and relationships between things. Put them all together, and almost any goal can be expressed as a verb (fasten), a noun (something), and a prepositional phrase (to a garbage can). Try it: Increase sales in Massachusetts, reduce vibrations in skis, and so on. By putting your goal in this format and playing with the hyponyms of each of its parts, you can explore diverse approaches to your problem in a simple and cost-effective way.

Here's how the approach worked when one of us (Jim) applied it to the real-world goal to reduce concussions in football. First he dropped the prepositional phrase "in football" from consideration and focused on the verb and noun: "reduce concussions." To break free of hidden assumptions, he used WordNet to rephrase the goal in as many different ways as possible: lessen trauma, weaken crash, soften jolt, reduce energy, absorb energy, minimize force, exchange forces, substitute energy, oppose energy, repel energy, lessen momentum, and so on. Using Google, he performed searches such as "concussions lessen trauma" to see which ways of phrasing the goal had been heavily explored already and which ones were under-explored.

Jim found that in the context of concussions, the phrase "repel energy" had relatively few search results—a sign that the solution it implied might have been overlooked. One way to repel energy is through magnets, and this suggested a possible approach: Make each helmet magnetic with the same pole so that two helmets would repel each other when in close proximity. Results from initial tests showed that when the helmets were about to collide, they decelerated, and because of their circular shape, they tended to glance off each other, as two magnetic billiard balls would, rather than smashing head-on. Several physicists have verified the plausibility of this approach for significantly reducing the force during helmet collisions.

We began the patenting process for our solution, but our lawyer discovered that someone had submitted the same idea just weeks earlier. We tip our hat to that person.

Visualizing Innovative Thinking

At its most basic level, problem solving consists of two connected activities: framing a goal and combining resources to accomplish it. Each variation of the goal, and every discovery of a "hidden" feature of an available resource, can suggest a different course to take. Our approach involves mapping the relationships among all the possibilities in a simple graph, somewhat analogous to a decision tree.

Starting with the goal at the top, we represent each refinement of the goal as a vector pointing downward. The available resources are placed at the bottom, with their features extending upward. Interactions among the resources and their features extend further toward the top. When the two sets of vectors connect, we have a "solution path." A solution path can be built by working from the top down, from the bottom up, or by switching back and forth between considering the goal and thinking about the resources.

This approach is an effective alternative to traditional brainstorming sessions for group innovation work, because it allows

---

Dominant survival strategy on the *Titanic*

The first step in discovering how resources could be used to reach a goal is to map the most obvious solution.

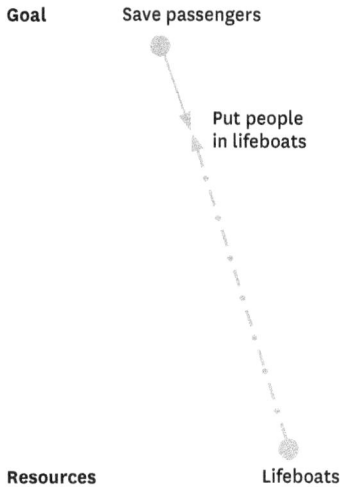

Goal   Save passengers

Put people
in lifeboats

Resources   Lifeboats

---

people to play to their strengths: Strategically oriented people can focus on refining the goal, while those more familiar with technologies and production processes can begin with the resources. We call this approach *brainswarming*—a nod to the concept of swarm intelligence. As people contribute to the growing graph, their activity resembles a swarm of insects.

To understand how this works, let's return to the problem facing the passengers on the *Titanic*. We'll start with the goal "save passengers." The most obvious resources are the lifeboats. The simplest application of the resources to achieve the goal is "put people in the lifeboats." Thus, we begin with a straight line (see the exhibit "Dominant survival strategy on the *Titanic*").

Next, we find different ways to phrase the goal to bring out different solutions. For instance, slightly different goals would be "keep

A Smarter Way to Brainstorm

WHEN PEOPLE GENERATE "brainswarming" graphs together, it's best for the group to work initially in silence, write contributions on sticky notes, and place the sticky notes at the proper place on the ever-growing graph. The benefits of silence include the following:

- The talkative few cannot dominate the session.

- There's no need for a facilitator to keep people from hijacking the discussion or judging others.

- People can work in parallel, so ideas are generated faster.

- No one needs to create a summary of the session. Take a picture of the graph and distribute it by email, or just keep the graph up on the wall for later use.

- There's no need to group similar ideas together, as you would in a traditional brainstorming session, because the grouping is done as the graph is built.

- Ideas are concise, since all contributions must fit on a sticky note.

- The silence allows people to move between thinking, writing down ideas, placing them on the graph, and building on one another's ideas.

- Top-down (big-picture) thinkers can work side by side with bottom-up (detail-oriented) thinkers.

- Fear of judgment from the boss or colleagues is reduced.

- There's no need for everyone to be present at the same time during the session. The graph can remain on the wall so that people can contribute at different times. Online brainswarming allows groups from around the world to work together remotely.

people warm and breathing" and "keep people out of the water." Let's look more closely at one of the options: keep people out of the water. One way is to place them on floating things—not just lifeboats—which might spark a fuller consideration of the resources at hand. You might remember that wood floats, for instance, suggesting that wooden tables might have been of help. Planks, or perhaps doors, from the ship might have been placed between the lifeboats to hold more people out of the water.

Overlooked strategies for saving *Titanic* passengers

Find new ways to name the goal, and new resources may present themselves.

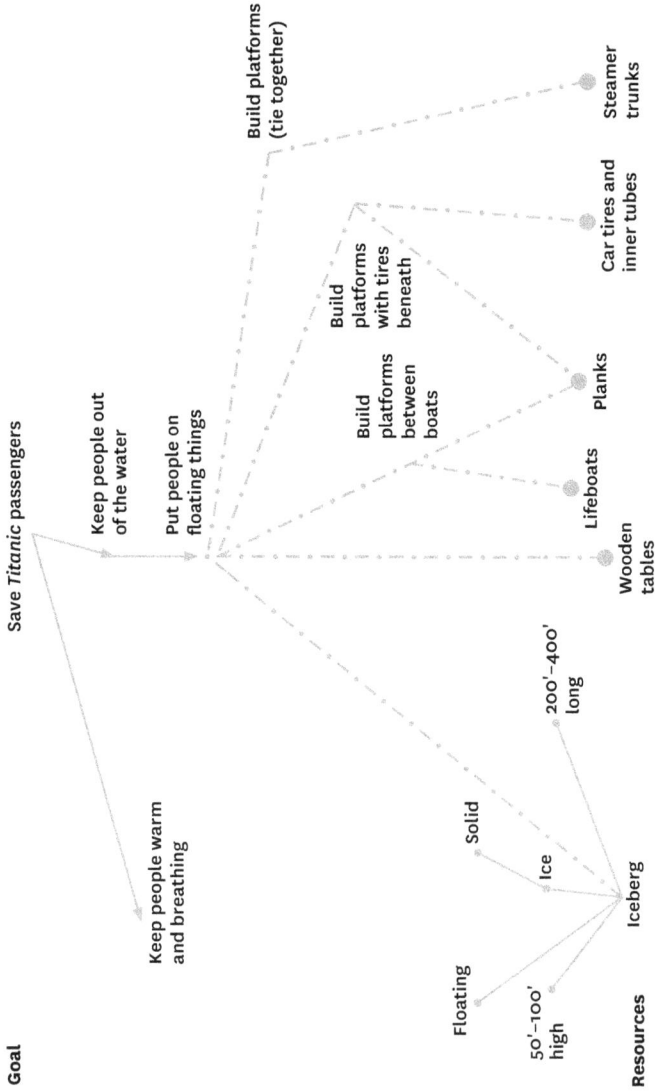

Goal

Save *Titanic* passengers

Keep people out of the water

Put people on floating things

Keep people warm and breathing

Build platforms (tie together)

Build platforms with tires beneath

Build platforms between boats

Resources

Floating

50'–100' high

Solid

Ice

200'–400' long

Iceberg

Wooden tables

Lifeboats

Planks

Car tires and inner tubes

Steamer trunks

Moving from floating things to even more-general considerations of buoyancy might bring to mind the many steamer trunks on board. Tying a set of trunks together to produce another sort of makeshift floating platform might have been enough to support several people directly or to provide a foundation upon which to build a more secure platform of wooden planks.

It was estimated that as many as 40 cars were on board. That means 160 tires and inner tubes (not to mention spare tires) were at passengers' disposal. Tying together rubber tires and inner tubes might conceivably have created a floating raft on which wooden boards could have been placed. And of course, the iceberg itself is a giant floating thing.

On that April night in 1912, none of these ideas might have worked, particularly since it took so long for people to understand the peril they were in. But the point of such an exercise is not to discover the "right solution"; it is to uncover as many connections between the goal and the widest view of the features of available resources as possible so that people look beyond the obvious.

The goal of the brainswarming graph, therefore, is to distill the problem-solving process to its most basic components and show how they are all related to one another. People do not have to remember all the components under consideration, because the graph shows them in a glance. This systematic approach takes some of the mystery out of innovation.

In our research, we are discovering that barriers to innovation are like gravity—pervasive, predictable, and not all that strong. There are many ways to overcome them, but the simplest and easiest path is to help your innovators notice what they're overlooking. Often it's right in front of their eyes.

Originally published in December 2015. Reprint R1512F

The Business Case for Curiosity

by Francesca Gino

MOST OF THE BREAKTHROUGH discoveries and remarkable inventions throughout history, from flints for starting a fire to self-driving cars, have something in common: They are the result of curiosity. The impulse to seek new information and experiences and explore novel possibilities is a basic human attribute. New research points to three important insights about curiosity as it relates to business. First, curiosity is much more important to an enterprise's performance than was previously thought. That's because cultivating it at all levels helps leaders and their employees adapt to uncertain market conditions and external pressures: When our curiosity is triggered, we think more deeply and rationally about decisions and come up with more creative solutions. In addition, curiosity allows leaders to gain more respect from their followers and inspires employees to develop more-trusting and more-collaborative relationships with colleagues.

Second, by making small changes to the design of their organizations and the ways they manage their employees, leaders can encourage curiosity—and improve their companies. This is true in every industry and for creative and routine work alike.

Third, although leaders might say they treasure inquisitive minds, in fact most stifle curiosity, fearing it will increase risk and inefficiency. In a survey I conducted of more than 3,000 employees from a wide range of firms and industries, only about 24% reported feeling curious in their jobs on a regular basis, and about 70% said they face barriers to asking more questions at work.

In this article I'll elaborate on the benefits of and common barriers to curiosity in the workplace and then offer five strategies that can help leaders get high returns on investments in employees' curiosity and in their own.

The Benefits of Curiosity

New research reveals a wide range of benefits for organizations, leaders, and employees.

Fewer decision-making errors

In my research I found that when our curiosity is triggered, we are less likely to fall prey to confirmation bias (looking for information that supports our beliefs rather than for evidence suggesting we are wrong) and to stereotyping people (making broad judgments, such as that women or minorities don't make good leaders). Curiosity has these positive effects because it leads us to generate alternatives.

More innovation and positive changes in both creative and noncreative jobs

Consider this example: In a field study INSEAD's Spencer Harrison and colleagues asked artisans selling their goods through an e-commerce website several questions aimed at assessing the curiosity they experience at work. After that, the participants' creativity was measured by the number of items they created and listed over a two-week period. A one-unit increase in curiosity (for instance, a score of 6 rather than 5 on a 7-point scale) was associated with 34% greater creativity.

In a separate study, Harrison and his colleagues focused on call centers, where jobs tend to be highly structured and turnover is generally high. They asked incoming hires at 10 organizations to complete a survey that, among other things, measured their curiosity before they began their new jobs. Four weeks in, the employees were surveyed about various aspects of their work. The results

Idea In Brief

The Problem

Leaders say they value employees who question or explore things, but research shows that they largely suppress curiosity, out of fear that it will increase risk and undermine efficiency.

Why This Matters

Curiosity improves engagement and collaboration. Curious people make better choices, improve their company's performance, and help their company adapt to uncertain market conditions and external pressures.

The Remedy

Leaders should encourage curiosity in themselves and others by making small changes to the design of their organization and the ways they manage their employees. Five strategies can guide them.

showed that the most curious employees sought the most information from coworkers, and the information helped them in their jobs—for instance, it boosted their creativity in addressing customers' concerns.

My own research confirms that encouraging people to be curious generates workplace improvements. For one study I recruited about 200 employees working in various companies and industries. Twice a week for four weeks, half of them received a text message at the start of their workday that read, "What is one topic or activity you are curious about today? What is one thing you usually take for granted that you want to ask about? Please make sure you ask a few 'Why questions' as you engage in your work throughout the day. Please set aside a few minutes to identify how you'll approach your work today with these questions in mind."

The other half (the control group) received a message designed to trigger reflection but not raise their curiosity: "What is one topic or activity you'll engage in today? What is one thing you usually work on or do that you'll also complete today? Please make sure you think about this as you engage in your work throughout the day. Please set aside a few minutes to identify how you'll approach your work today with these questions in mind."

After four weeks, the participants in the first group scored higher than the others on questions assessing their innovative behaviors at work, such as whether they had made constructive suggestions for implementing solutions to pressing organizational problems.

When we are curious, we view tough situations more creatively. Studies have found that curiosity is associated with less defensive reactions to stress and less aggressive reactions to provocation. We also perform better when we're curious. In a study of 120 employees I found that natural curiosity was associated with better job performance, as evaluated by their direct bosses.

Reduced group conflict

My research found that curiosity encourages members of a group to put themselves in one another's shoes and take an interest in one another's ideas rather than focus only on their own perspective. That causes them to work together more effectively and smoothly: Conflicts are less heated, and groups achieve better results.

More-open communication and better team performance

Working with executives in a leadership program at Harvard Kennedy School, my colleagues and I divided participants into groups of five or six, had some groups participate in a task that heightened their curiosity, and then asked all the groups to engage in a simulation that tracked performance. The groups whose curiosity had been heightened performed better than the control groups because they shared information more openly and listened more carefully.

Two Barriers to Curiosity

Despite the well-established benefits of curiosity, organizations often discourage it. This is not because leaders don't see its value. On the contrary, both leaders and employees understand that curiosity creates positive outcomes for their companies. In the survey of more than 3,000 employees mentioned earlier, 92% credited curious people with bringing new ideas into teams and organizations and viewed curiosity as a catalyst for job satisfaction, motivation, innovation, and high performance.

Yet executives' actions often tell a different story. True, some organizations, including 3M and Facebook, give employees free time to pursue their interests, but they are rare. And even in such organizations, employees often have challenging short-term performance goals (such as meeting a quarterly sales target or launching a new product by a certain date) that consume the "free time" they could have spent exploring alternative approaches to their work or coming up with innovative ideas.

Two tendencies restrain leaders from encouraging curiosity:

They have the wrong mindset about exploration

Leaders often think that letting employees follow their curiosity will lead to a costly mess. In a recent survey I conducted of 520 chief learning officers and chief talent development officers, I found that they often shy away from encouraging curiosity because they believe the company would be harder to manage if people were allowed to explore their own interests. They also believe that disagreements would arise and making and executing decisions would slow down, raising the cost of doing business. Research finds that although people list creativity as a goal, they frequently reject creative ideas when actually presented with them. That's understandable: Exploration often involves questioning the status quo and doesn't always produce useful information. But it also means not settling for the first possible solution—and so it often yields better remedies.

They seek efficiency to the detriment of exploration

In the early 1900s Henry Ford focused all his efforts on one goal: reducing production costs to create a car for the masses. By 1908 he had realized that vision with the introduction of the Model T. Demand grew so high that by 1921 the company was producing 56% of all passenger cars in the United States—a remarkable success made possible primarily by the firm's efficiency-centered model of work. But in the late 1920s, as the U.S. economy rose to new heights, consumers started wanting greater variety in their cars. While Ford remained fixated on improving the Model T, competitors such as General Motors started producing an array of models and soon captured the main share of the market. Owing to its single-minded focus on efficiency, Ford stopped experimenting and innovating and fell behind.

These leadership tendencies help explain why our curiosity usually declines the longer we're in a job. In one survey, I asked about 250 people who had recently started working for various companies a series of questions designed to measure curiosity; six months later I administered a follow-up survey. Although initial levels of curiosity varied, after six months everyone's curiosity had dropped, with the average decline exceeding 20%. Because people were under pressure to complete their work quickly, they had little time to ask questions about broad processes or overall goals.

Five Ways to Bolster Curiosity

It takes thought and discipline to stop stifling curiosity and start fostering it. Here are five strategies leaders can employ.

1. Hire for curiosity

In 2004 an anonymous billboard appeared on Highway 101, in the heart of Silicon Valley, posing this puzzle: "{first 10-digit prime found in consecutive digits of e}.com." The answer, 7427466391.com, led the curious online, where they found another equation to solve. The handful of people who did so were invited to submit a résumé to Google. The company took this unusual approach to finding job candidates because it places a premium on curiosity. (People didn't even need to be engineers!) As Eric Schmidt, Google's CEO from 2001 to 2011, has said, "We run this company on questions, not answers."

Google also identifies naturally curious people through interview questions such as these: "Have you ever found yourself unable to stop learning something you've never encountered before? Why? What kept you persistent?" The answers usually highlight either a specific purpose driving the candidate's inquiry ("It was my job to find the answer") or genuine curiosity ("I just had to figure out the answer").

IDEO, the design and consulting company, seeks to hire "T-shaped" employees: people with deep skills that allow them to contribute to the creative process (the vertical stroke of the T) and a predisposition for collaboration across disciplines, a quality requiring empathy and curiosity (the horizontal stroke of the T). The firm understands that empathy and curiosity are related: Empathy allows employees to listen thoughtfully and see problems or decisions from another person's perspective, while curiosity extends to interest in other people's disciplines, so much so that one may start to practice them. And it recognizes that most people perform at their best not because they're specialists but because their deep skill is accompanied by an intellectual curiosity that leads them to ask questions, explore, and collaborate.

To identify potential employees who are T-shaped, IDEO pays attention to how candidates talk about past projects. Someone who focuses only on his or her own contributions may lack the breadth to appreciate collaboration. T-shaped candidates are more likely to talk about how they succeeded with the help of others and to express interest in working collaboratively on future projects.

To assess curiosity, employers can also ask candidates about their interests outside of work. Reading books unrelated to one's own field and exploring questions just for the sake of knowing the answers are indications of curiosity. And companies can administer curiosity assessments, which have been validated in a myriad of studies. These generally measure whether people explore things they don't know, analyze data to uncover new ideas, read widely beyond their field, have diverse interests outside work, and are excited by learning opportunities.

It's also important to remember that the questions candidates ask—not just the answers they provide—can signal curiosity. For instance, people who want to know about aspects of the organization that aren't directly related to the job at hand probably have more natural curiosity than people who ask only about the role they would perform.

2. Model inquisitiveness

Leaders can encourage curiosity throughout their organizations by being inquisitive themselves. In 2000, when Greg Dyke had been named director general of the BBC but hadn't yet assumed the position, he spent five months visiting the BBC's major locations, assembling the staff at each stop. Employees expected a long presentation but instead got a simple question: "What is the one thing I should do to make things better for you?" Dyke would listen carefully and then ask, "What is the one thing I should do to make things better for our viewers and listeners?"

The BBC's employees respected their new boss for taking the time to ask questions and listen. Dyke used their responses to inform his thinking about the changes needed to solve problems facing the BBC and to identify what to work on first. After officially taking the reins, he gave a speech to the staff that reflected what he had learned and showed employees that he had been truly interested in what they said.

By asking questions and genuinely listening to the responses, Dyke modeled the importance of those behaviors. He also highlighted the fact that when we are exploring new terrain, listening is as important as talking: It helps us fill gaps in our knowledge and identify other questions to investigate.

That may seem intuitive, but my research shows that we often prefer to talk rather than to listen with curiosity. For instance, when I asked some 230 high-level leaders in executive education classes what they would do if confronted with an organizational crisis stemming from both financial and cultural issues, most said they would take action: move to stop the financial bleeding and introduce initiatives to refresh the culture. Only a few said they would ask questions rather than simply impose their ideas on others. Management books commonly encourage leaders assuming new positions to communicate their vision from the start rather than ask employees how they can be most helpful. It's bad advice.

Why do we refrain from asking questions? Because we fear we'll be judged incompetent, indecisive, or unintelligent. Plus, time is precious, and we don't want to bother people. Experience and expertise exacerbate the problem: As people climb the organizational ladder, they think they have less to learn. Leaders also tend to believe they're expected to talk and provide answers, not ask questions.

Such fears and beliefs are misplaced, my recent research shows. When we demonstrate curiosity about others by asking questions, people like us *more* and view us as *more* competent, and the heightened trust makes our relationships more interesting and intimate. By asking questions, we promote more-meaningful connections and more-creative outcomes.

Another way leaders can model curiosity is by acknowledging when they don't know the answer; that makes it clear that it's OK to be guided by curiosity. Patricia Fili-Krushel told me that when she joined WebMD Health as chief executive, she met with a group of male engineers in Silicon Valley. They were doubtful that she could add value to their work and, right off the bat, asked what she knew about engineering. Without hesitation, Fili-Krushel made a zero with her fingers. "This is how much I know about engineering," she told them. "However, I do know how to run businesses, and I'm hoping you can teach me what I need to know about your world." When leaders concede that they don't have the answer to a question, they show that they value the process of looking for answers and motivate others to explore as well.

New hires at Pixar Animation Studios are often hesitant to question the status quo, given the company's track record of hit movies and the brilliant work of those who have been there for years. To combat that tendency, Ed Catmull, the cofounder and president, makes a point of talking about times when Pixar made bad choices. Like all other organizations, he says, Pixar is not perfect, and it needs fresh eyes to spot opportunities for improvement (see "How Pixar Fosters Collective Creativity," page 33). In this way Catmull gives new recruits license to question existing practices. Recognizing the limits of our own knowledge and skills sends a powerful signal to others.

Tenelle Porter, a postdoctoral scholar in psychology at the University of California, Davis, describes intellectual humility as the ability to acknowledge that what we know is sharply limited. As her research demonstrates, higher levels of intellectual humility are associated with a greater willingness to consider views other than our own. People with more intellectual humility also do better in school and at work. Why? When we accept that our own knowledge is finite, we are more apt to see that the world is always changing and that the future will diverge from the present. By embracing this insight, leaders and employees can begin to recognize the power of exploration.

Finally, leaders can model inquisitiveness by approaching the unknown with curiosity rather than judgment. Bob Langer, who heads one of MIT's most productive laboratories, told me recently that this principle guides how he manages his staff. As human beings, we all feel an urge to evaluate others—often not positively. We're quick to judge their ideas, behaviors, and perspectives, even when those relate to things that haven't been tried before. Langer avoids this trap by raising questions about others' ideas, which leads people to think more deeply about their perspective and to remain curious about the tough problems they are trying to tackle. In doing so, he is modeling behavior that he expects of others in the lab.

3. Emphasize learning goals

When I asked Captain Chesley "Sully" Sullenberger how he was able to land a commercial aircraft safely in the Hudson River, he described his passion for continuous learning. Although commercial flights are almost always routine, every time his plane pushed back from the gate he would remind himself that he needed to be prepared for the unexpected. "What can I learn?" he would think. When the unexpected came to pass, on a cold January day in 2009, Sully was able to ask himself what he *could* do, given the available options, and come up with a creative solution. He successfully fought the tendency to grasp for the most obvious option (landing at the nearest airport). Especially when under pressure, we narrow in on what immediately seems the best course of action. But those who are passionate about continuous learning contemplate a wide range of options and perspectives. As the accident report shows, Sully carefully considered several alternatives in the 208 seconds between his discovery that the aircraft's engines lacked thrust and his landing of the plane in the Hudson.

It's natural to concentrate on results, especially in the face of tough challenges. But focusing on learning is generally more beneficial to us and our organizations, as some landmark studies show. For example, when U.S. Air Force personnel were given a demanding goal for the number of planes to be landed in a set time frame, their performance *decreased*. Similarly, in a study led by Southern Methodist University's Don VandeWalle, sales professionals who were naturally focused on performance goals, such as meeting their targets and being seen by colleagues as good at their jobs, did worse during a promotion of a product (a piece of medical equipment priced at about $5,400) than reps who were naturally focused on learning goals, such as exploring how to be a better salesperson. That cost them, because the company awarded a bonus of $300 for each unit sold.

A body of research demonstrates that framing work around learning goals (developing competence, acquiring skills, mastering new situations, and so on) rather than performance goals (hitting targets, proving our competence, impressing others) boosts motivation. And when motivated by learning goals, we acquire more-diverse skills, do better at work, get higher grades in college, do better on problem-solving tasks, and receive higher ratings after training. Unfortunately, organizations often prioritize performance goals.

Leaders can help employees adopt a learning mindset by communicating the importance of learning and by rewarding people not only for their performance but for the learning needed to get there. Deloitte took this path: In 2013 it replaced its performance management system with one that tracks both learning and performance. Employees meet regularly with a coach to discuss their development and learning along with the support they need to continually grow.

Leaders can also stress the value of learning by reacting positively to ideas that may be mediocre in themselves but could be springboards to better ones. Writers and directors at Pixar are trained in a technique called "plussing," which involves building on ideas without using judgmental language. Instead of rejecting a sketch, for example, a director might find a starting point by saying, "I like Woody's eyes, and what if we . . . ?" Someone else might jump in with another "plus." This technique allows people to remain curious, listen actively, respect the ideas of others, and contribute their own. By promoting a process that allows all sorts of ideas to be explored, leaders send a clear message that learning is a key goal even if it doesn't always lead to success.

4. Let employees explore and broaden their interests
Organizations can foster curiosity by giving employees time and resources to explore their interests. One of my favorite examples comes from my native country. It involves Italy's first typewriter factory, Olivetti, founded in 1908 in the foothills of the Italian Alps. In the 1930s some employees caught a coworker leaving the factory with a bag full of iron pieces and machinery. They accused him of stealing and asked the company to fire him. The worker told the CEO, Adriano Olivetti, that he was taking the parts home to work on a new machine over the weekend because he didn't have time while performing his regular job. Instead of firing him, Olivetti gave him time to create the machine and charged him with overseeing its production. The result was Divisumma, the first electronic calculator. Divisumma sold well worldwide in the 1950s and 1960s, and Olivetti promoted the worker to technical director. Unlike leaders who would have shown him the door, Olivetti gave him the space to explore his curiosity, with remarkable results.

Some organizations provide resources to support employees' outside interests. Since 1996 the manufacturing conglomerate United Technologies (UTC) has given as much as $12,000 in tuition annually to any employee seeking a degree part-time—no strings attached. Leaders often don't want to invest in training employees for fear that they will jump to a competitor and take their expensively acquired skills with them. Even though UTC hasn't tried to quantify the benefits of its tuition reimbursement program, Gail Jackson, the vice president of human resources when we spoke, believes in the importance of curious employees. "It's better to train and have them leave than not to train and have them stay," she told me. But according to the Society for Human Resource Management's 2017 employee benefits report, only 44% of organizations provide or support cross-training to develop skills not directly related to workers' jobs.

Leaders might provide opportunities for employees to travel to unfamiliar locales. When we have chances to expand our interests, research has found, we not only remain curious but also become more confident about what we can accomplish and more successful at work. Employees can "travel" to other roles and areas of the organization to gain a broader perspective. At Pixar, employees across the organization can provide "notes"—questions and advice—that help directors consider all sorts of possibilities for the movies they are working on.

Employees can also broaden their interests by broadening their networks. Curious people often end up being star performers thanks to their diverse networks, my research with the University of Toronto's Tiziana Casciaro, Bill McEvily, and Evelyn Zhang finds. Because they're more comfortable than others asking questions, such people more easily create and nurture ties at work—and those ties are critical to their career development and success. The organization benefits when employees are connected to people who can help them with challenges and motivate them to go the extra mile. MIT's Bob Langer works to raise curiosity in his students by introducing them to experts in his network. Similarly, by connecting people across organizational departments and units, leaders can encourage employees to be curious about their colleagues' work and ways of doing business.

Deliberate thinking about work spaces can broaden networks and encourage the cross-pollination of ideas. In the 1990s, when Pixar was designing a new home for itself in Emeryville, across the bay from San Francisco, the initial plans called for a separate building for each department. But then-owner Steve Jobs had concerns about isolating the various departments and decided to build a single structure with a large atrium in the center, containing employee mailboxes, a café, a gift shop, and screening rooms. Forcing employees to interact, he reasoned, would expose them to one another's work and ideas.

Leaders can also boost employees' curiosity by carefully designing their teams. Consider Massimo Bottura, the owner of Osteria Francescana, a three-Michelin-star restaurant in Modena, Italy, that was rated the Best Restaurant in the World in 2016 and 2018. His sous-chefs are Davide di Fabio, from Italy, and Kondo Takahiko, from Japan. The two differ not only in their origins but also in their strengths: Di Fabio is more comfortable with improvisation, while Takahiko is obsessed with precision. Such "collisions" make the kitchen more innovative, Bottura believes, and inspire curiosity in other workers.

5. Have "Why?" "What if . . . ?" and "How might we . . . ?" days
The inspiration for the Polaroid instant camera was a three-year-old's question. Inventor Edwin Land's daughter was impatient to see a photo her father had just snapped. When he explained that the film had to be processed, she wondered aloud, "Why do we have to wait for the picture?"

As every parent knows, *Why?* is ubiquitous in the vocabulary of young children, who have an insatiable need to understand the world around them. They aren't afraid to ask questions, and they don't worry about whether others believe they should already know the answers. But as children grow older, self-consciousness creeps in, along with the desire to appear confident and demonstrate expertise. By the time we're adults, we often suppress our curiosity.

Leaders can help draw out our innate curiosity. One company I visited asked all employees for "What if . . . ?" and "How might we . . . ?" questions about the firm's goals and plans. They came up with all sorts of things, which were discussed and evaluated. As a concrete sign that questioning was supported and rewarded, the best questions were displayed on banners hung on the walls. Some of the questions led employees to suggest ideas for how to work more effectively. (For more on the importance of asking good questions before seeking solutions, see "Better Brainstorming," HBR, March–April 2018).

In one study, my colleagues and I asked adults working in a wide range of jobs and industries to read one of two sets of materials on three organizational elements: goals, roles, and how organizations as a whole work together. For half the workers, the information was presented as the "grow method"—our version of a control condition. We encouraged that group to view those elements as immutable, and we stressed the importance of following existing processes that managers had already defined. For the other half, the information was presented as the "go back method." We encouraged those employees to see the elements as fluid and to "go back" and rethink them. A week later we found that the workers who'd read about the "go back method" showed more creativity in tasks than the workers in the "grow method" group. They were more open to others' ideas and worked more effectively with one another.

To encourage curiosity, leaders should also teach employees how to ask good questions. Bob Langer has said he wants to "help people make the transition from giving good answers to asking good questions" (see "The Edison of Medicine," HBR, March–April 2017). He also tells his students that they could change the world, thus boosting the curiosity they need to tackle challenging problems.

Organizing "Why?" days, when employees are encouraged to ask that question if facing a challenge, can go a long way toward fostering curiosity. Intellectual Ventures, a company that generates inventions and buys and licenses patents, organizes "invention sessions" in which people from different disciplines, backgrounds, and levels of expertise come together to discuss potential solutions to tough problems, which helps them consider issues from various angles (see "Funding Eureka!" HBR, March 2010). Similarly, under Toyota's 5 Whys approach, employees are asked to investigate problems by asking Why? After coming up with an answer, they are to ask why *that's* the case, and so on until they have asked the question five times. This mindset can help employees innovate by challenging existing perspectives.

In most organizations, leaders and employees alike receive the implicit message that asking questions is an unwanted challenge to authority. They are trained to focus on their work without looking closely at the process or their overall goals. But maintaining a sense of wonder is crucial to creativity and innovation. The most effective leaders look for ways to nurture their employees' curiosity to fuel learning and discovery.

Originally published in September–October 2018. Reprint R1805B

Bring Your Breakthrough Ideas to Life

by Cyril Bouquet, Jean-Louis Barsoux, and Michael Wade

IN 2003 THE Indian environmental researcher Narayana Peesapaty spotted an alarming trend: Groundwater levels in the region of Hyderabad were falling precipitously. He examined rainfall records but found nothing to explain the drop. Looking deeper, he discovered that the culprit was a change in agricultural practices. Many area farmers had abandoned millet—a traditional crop increasingly regarded as "the poor man's food"—in favor of rice, a thirsty crop that requires 60 times as much water to grow. And because they had access to heavily subsidized electricity, the farmers were continuously pumping water into their fields.

Peesapaty tried to influence agricultural policies by documenting the problem in government reports, to no avail. So he looked instead for ways to boost demand for millet. He hit on the idea of turning it into "edible cutlery"—a solution that could attack not just the groundwater deficit but also the scourge of plastic waste. Peesapaty quit his job to pursue the project. A decade later, after a video he posted about the cutlery went viral, orders began pouring in. Two crowdfunding campaigns exceeded their targets by more than twelvefold, and the first corporate orders shipped in 2016. It's too soon to know whether groundwater levels have stabilized. But many farmers have already resumed growing the more sustainable crop, and to further boost production, the government declared 2018 the National Year of Millets.

As Peesapaty's story demonstrates, there are two potential routes to any solution: *conformity* (in this case, trying to use established channels to affect policy) and *originality*. The first is adequate for many everyday challenges. But for thornier problems, more-divergent thinking may be required.

As academics with a long-standing interest in attention, sense making, innovation, and digital transformation, we have spent the past decade researching pioneering thinkers and changemakers in a wide range of fields, from entrepreneurs to medics to chefs. Our work with corporate clients has included running top-team innovation workshops, leading full-scale acceleration programs, and orchestrating enormous transformation journeys. We have also interviewed and surveyed hundreds of executives involved in innovation efforts. Through these efforts we have identified recurrent patterns in the evolution of breakthrough ideas and constructed a five-part framework for developing them and ensuring their survival.

Unconventional thinkers focus their attention closely and with fresh eyes, step back to gain perspective, imagine unorthodox combinations, experiment quickly and smartly, and navigate potentially hostile environments outside and within their organizations. The challenge throughout is to overcome biases and mental models that may constrain creativity or doom a great idea.

In this article we'll describe the five elements of the framework and explore how digital tools can augment them. But first let's look at why game-changing innovation remains so difficult despite organizational and societal pressure for transformative results.

The Elusiveness of Breakthrough Innovations

The digital advances of the past two decades have enabled a much broader population than ever before to express creative intelligence. Unconventional thinkers the world over have unprecedented access to the distributed knowledge, talents, capital, and consumers they

Idea in Brief

The Problem

Despite recent digital advances and an improved understanding of the innovation process, game-changing offerings remain hard to come by.

Why It Happens

Existing innovation models are unrealistic and often incomplete, failing to incorporate the digital aspect of innovation and emphasizing speed over deep reflection. They gloss over pitfalls and biases and may focus so intensely on users that other key stakeholders are neglected.

The Remedy

Five practices can help bring breakthrough ideas to fruition: Attend closely and with fresh eyes, step back to gain perspective, imagine unorthodox combinations, experiment quickly and smartly, and navigate potentially hostile environments both inside and outside the company.

need to create a start-up or a movement around a great idea. Innovation has been thoroughly democratized.

And yet breakthrough offerings remain hard to come by. Apart from the transformation of services powered by mobile apps and the internet, we have not seen spectacular surges of innovation across sectors. The economists Tyler Cowen and Robert Gordon have spoken of innovation stagnation. The business thinker Gary Hamel notes that corporations are awash in ideas that fall into one of two buckets: incremental no-brainer or flaky no-hoper. And in our consulting work with innovation teams we see many promising ideas become superficial, narrow, or skewed—or perish altogether.

The lack of progress is surprising given that companies have an improved understanding of the innovation process, driven in large part by design thinking and lean start-up methodologies. Terms such as "user centered," "ideation," and "pivot" have become commonplace and have changed the way business leaders think about creating new offerings. Yet for all this guidance, only 43% of corporations have what experts consider a well-defined process for innovation, according to the research firm CB Insights.

When we talk with entrepreneurs and executives about existing innovation frameworks, their criticisms center on three overlapping issues. First, the models are *unrealistic:* The still-influential waterfall, or stage-gate approach, for example, is overly linear, with little regard for the constant zigzagging between activities that may be called for. Elmar Mock, a serial entrepreneur who co-created the Swatch, put it this way in a 2016 podcast: "The very natural instinct for an innovator is to move in a nonlinear way, to go from concepts to know-how back to concept, to relook for new know-how, to change the concept again." Second, the models are *incomplete:* They don't incorporate the digital aspect of innovation or show how it relates to the "humancentric" principles enshrined in design thinking. They emphasize action and fast iteration (pillars of the lean start-up methodology), but in doing so they tend to downplay what Wharton's Adam Grant calls strategic procrastination—allowing yourself time for deep reflection. Third, the models are *misleading:* They gloss over the pitfalls and biases that may constrain creativity. And by focusing so intensely on users, they minimize the roles of other stakeholders and the need for inventiveness in mobilizing support to establish and deploy novel offerings.

Regarding this last point, executives recognize that to devise ingenious innovations, they must break paradigms and shift mindsets—but when it comes to delivery, they often lapse into standard ways of thinking. Consider the failed Sony Reader. All the creativity that went into its development was undone by a lack of originality in execution. Sony neglected to enlist the book publishing industry as an ally—a mistake Amazon did not make when it launched the technically inferior but hugely successful Kindle, 14 months later. To make your stellar innovation thrive, approach unconventional partners, identify underutilized channels, and invent new business models. Put as much creative energy into introducing and delivering offerings as you did into generating them. Sony engineered an elegant *device,* but Amazon designed an original *solution.*

Our framework complements design thinking, lean start-up, the business model canvas, and other innovation strategies. It is more accepting of the messiness inherent in developing a truly breakthrough solution, recognizing that the activities involved relate to one another in unpredictable, nonlinear ways. The elements of our framework are not unique, but collectively they capture the full scope and reality of the innovation process, including the critical role of reflection in conceiving opportunities and the level of organizational reinvention needed in the final push to market.

Let's turn now to those five elements.

Attention: Look Through a Fresh Lens

Attention is the act of focusing closely on a given context to understand its dynamics and latent needs. The trouble is that expertise often interferes, directing people's attention and unconsciously blinding them to radical insights. The French call this *déformation profession-nelle:* the tendency to observe reality through the distorting lens of one's job or training. To combat that bias, question what perspective drives your attention and what you may be missing as a result.

Take the case of Billy Fischer, a U.S. infectious disease expert who regularly traveled to rural Guinea to fight the Ebola epidemic. In May 2014 he saw that the recommended approach was not working: The local treatment facility was focused on containing the spread by isolating anyone exposed to the virus, but people were hiding to avoid being quarantined. Talking with patients, Fischer realized that the problem was fear: The mortality rate for patients in quarantine was 90%—so people understandably saw it as a death sentence. He insisted that the clinic prioritize patient recovery instead. Testing new treatment combinations, he and his colleagues slashed mortality rates to 50%, reversing the negative perception of quarantine and thus helping to stem the contagion.

By setting aside your preconceptions, you become a sharper observer of what people say and do. This changes not just *how* you pay attention but also *whom* you pay attention to—and previously unconsidered niche populations often reveal unsuspected pain points. The toy group Lego learns a lot from the frustrations of its adult enthusiasts, the cleaning-products giant S.C. Johnson from observing hygiene-obsessed OCD sufferers, and IKEA from trying to understand what "IKEA hackers," who customize and repurpose the furniture maker's goods, are "trying to tell us about our own products."

How robust is your creative process?

To assess your capacity to innovate, answer the following questions and calculate your average score for each element. Scores below 4 indicate areas for improvement.

Attention — Disagree ————→ Agree

	1	2	3	4	5	6	7
I periodically try to experience what it feels like to be a user/customer.	1	2	3	4	5	6	7
I notice subtle developments or surprising things that others have overlooked.	1	2	3	4	5	6	7
I use digital tools to constantly monitor my environment.	1	2	3	4	5	6	7
I am curious about customers who behave in very different ways.	1	2	3	4	5	6	7

Perspective

	1	2	3	4	5	6	7
I make time to consider the big picture, even when I am deep in details.	1	2	3	4	5	6	7
I attend events that have nothing to do with my core industry.	1	2	3	4	5	6	7
I try to challenge my default perspective on problems.	1	2	3	4	5	6	7
I seek out people with a different view on the issues I am looking at.	1	2	3	4	5	6	7

Digital technologies allow the tracking of behavior on a much larger scale than was previously possible, offering complementary ways of detecting tacit needs. In health care, for instance, researchers are studying the lived experience of Parkinson's disease by having volunteers use their smartphones to measure tremors (thanks to the function that captures portrait and landscape views), muscle tone (the microphone indicates the strength of the patient's voice box), involuntary movements (the touch screen records them), and gait (if the phone is in a pocket, it senses the patient's unsteadiness). The researchers can thus track the efficacy of medication not just before and after dosing but over time. And they get a rich picture of what participants actually do, as opposed to what they say they do.

Imagination							
I openly question accepted practices and assumptions.	1	2	3	4	5	6	7
I mix ideas from unrelated areas.	1	2	3	4	5	6	7
I try to be creative in how I make connections between things I observe.	1	2	3	4	5	6	7
Experimentation							
I try to find novel ways of demonstrating the value of my ideas.	1	2	3	4	5	6	7
I use computer simulations to test the feasibility of my ideas.	1	2	3	4	5	6	7
I often don't settle on the first solution I come up with, or the second.	1	2	3	4	5	6	7
I allow myself to fail as long as I learn from it.	1	2	3	4	5	6	7
Navigation							
I have access to people who can help champion my solution.	1	2	3	4	5	6	7
I fully understand the varying interests of critical stakeholders.	1	2	3	4	5	6	7
I know how to tailor and deliver a message for different audiences.	1	2	3	4	5	6	7
I have a good sense of when to disclose strategic information.	1	2	3	4	5	6	7

Cyberspace can also help companies identify expert users in their practice communities. Medical device companies could glean insights from the online forums of "body hackers"—people who implant microchips, magnets, LED lights, and other technology in themselves with the aim of augmenting human capabilities. Inspired by that ethos, Medtronic is considering how its pill-sized pacemaker could be enhanced and implanted in healthy people to give them biometric feedback and improve their lifelong care.

Companies can use digital technology to engage with trendsetters directly or eavesdrop on user forums and blogs for clues about evolving needs. In 2009 Nivea conducted an online analysis, or "netnography," of discussions about deodorant use across 200 social media sites. Contrary to expectations, the key preoccupation was not fragrance, effectiveness, or irritation but the staining of clothes. This insight paved the way for a new category of antistain deodorants in 2011, the most successful launch in the company's 130-year history. In the public sector, online media analysis is being used to explore issues such as exercise, generic drugs, and—in an effort to improve health care social workers' interventions—resistance to vaccination.

Digital technologies can't replace direct observation, of course. But they expand the number and type of insights generated, providing access to a wealth of unfiltered and unstructured user-generated content that people can then make sense of.

Perspective: Step Back to Expand Your Understanding

Having zoomed in to gather insights about a situation, a need, or a challenge, you must then pull out to gain perspective, fighting against framing and action biases that might encourage you to accept the issue as presented and rush into problem solving. To process what you have learned, detach: Change activities, or take a strategic break. During his third attempt to circle the globe by balloon, in 1999, the Swiss psychiatrist and adventurer Bertrand Piccard was obsessed by fuel conservation. After completing the exploit, with barely any liquid gas to spare, he realized that he had spent his 20 days aloft in constant fear of running out. As he waited (for half a day) to be picked up from the Egyptian desert, it dawned on him that the core problem was not how to manage fuel but how to manage *without* fuel. Redefining the issue in this way set the stage for his next circumnavigation challenge—in a fully solar-powered plane.

His insight occurred only after Piccard stepped back. It's not easy to prime yourself for inspiration while you're in the thick of action. Consider the pioneering chef Ferran Adrià, who melded haute cuisine, art, and science; generated more than 1,800 signature dishes over 20 years; and earned his restaurant, El Bulli, the rating of "world's best" a record five times. The key to his creativity, Adrià once explained to HBR, was closing his restaurant for six months each year. "The pressure to serve every day doesn't offer the kind of tranquility necessary to create as we would like," he said. "The most important thing is to leave time for regeneration." This mindset is reflected in the Japanese concept *ma,* which stresses that space is necessary for growth and enlightenment.

Digital tools can help create that space, freeing up your time through automation. They also amplify weak signals, making it easier to see patterns. For example, take the case of DoSomething, a global nonprofit that works with young people to effect social change and mobilizes its massive community of volunteers by text. Along with messages from people looking to donate their time—some 200,000 messages in a typical campaign—incoming texts would include a handful of unrelated messages from distressed teenagers. Staffers would respond with referrals to relevant helplines—until one particularly disturbing message, from a girl being raped by her father, forced them to rethink their approach.

After two weeks of sleepless nights for DoSomething's leadership, they realized why adolescents were contacting the organization with problems unrelated to its cause: Texting is anonymous, private, and quiet. The cries for help pointed to an unmet need, leading to the creation of a spin-off organization—Crisis Text Line (CTL), a free service that offers round-the-clock counseling and intervention. Although launched without fanfare, it has outpaced even Facebook's reach throughout the United States.

Imagination: Look for Unexpected Combinations

To produce a truly original idea, you must free your imagination, challenge orthodoxy, and envision that which is not. But "functional fixedness" often limits the ability to think creatively or to conceive of alternative uses for familiar objects and concepts. Overcoming this barrier requires asking uninhibited questions such as "Why not?" and "What if?"—as Van Phillips did when he queried the requirement that prosthetic limbs resemble human ones. His now-familiar C-shaped blades help amputees run and jump much the way able-bodied athletes do.

To spur imagination, organizations may ask questions such as "What if we no longer did what we do now?"—not necessarily because they intend to abandon current activities but as a way to envision connections between existing strengths and new opportunities. In 2009 the McLaren Group, known for Formula 1 racing, asked precisely that question—which liberated it to think about how its capabilities in materials science, aerodynamics, simulation, predictive analytics, and teamwork might apply to other sectors. It leveraged those capabilities to improve the performance of clients ranging from elite rowing, cycling, and sailing teams to health care systems and air traffic control services. As a result, it has morphed into a consulting and technology group that happens to have a successful Formula 1 team.

Imagination is often seen as something mystical and inaccessible, but it is chiefly a matter of positing unexpected combinations. At the most basic level, you can apply an existing solution from one domain to another. Jonathan Ledgard, a war reporter and a former longtime Africa correspondent for the *Economist,* imagined a drone-based network for delivering medical supplies to remote areas in Africa. Thus was born Redline, which began trial operations in Rwanda in 2016. Because the price and efficiency of drone batteries has not kept pace with advances in airframes, Ledgard has begun to focus on developing droneports to support the air cargo routes.

Outsiders often find it easier than insiders do to connect disparate thoughts, because they come to the table with fewer preconceptions. Phillips was not an engineer and had never worked in a prosthetics lab; his running blades were inspired by his experience as a pole vaulter and a springboard diver prior to losing a leg in an accident. The latest medical innovation for assisting difficult births—successfully tested in South America and recently licensed by Becton, Dickinson—was the brainchild of an Argentinian car mechanic, Jorge Odón. Enthralled by a YouTube video on using a plastic bag to retrieve a cork from inside an empty wine bottle, the father of five realized that the same principle could save a baby stuck in the birth canal. As a chief medic at the World Health Organization told a *New York Times* reporter, "An obstetrician would have tried to improve the forceps or the vacuum extractor, but obstructed labor needed a mechanic."

Research confirms that distance often helps in coming up with novel ideas. In one study, separate groups of carpenters, roofers, and in-line skaters were asked for ideas on how to improve the design of carpenters' respirator masks, roofers' safety belts, and skaters' kneepads. Each group was much better at coming up with solutions for the fields outside its own.

Organizations try to spark such connections by bringing together people with diverse knowledge bases and perspectives. Technology allows them to tap the wisdom of experts far beyond their networks—people who may have no familiarity with a given market or industry but can bring different experiences to bear. For example, in 2007 the Oil Spill Recovery Institute used crowdsourcing to tackle the long-standing problem of cleaning up oil spills in subarctic waters. The winning idea came not from an oil industry specialist but from a chemist, John Davis, who applied his expertise in the concrete industry to devise a means of keeping oil liquid as it is pumped. Examining 166 problem-solving contests posted on the InnoCentive innovation platform, Harvard Business School's Karim Lakhani found that winning entries were more likely to come from "unexpected contributors" with "distant fields" of expertise.

In addition, the digital revolution has blurred industry boundaries, facilitating unexpected combinations. The data routinely collected in one area can benefit players in unrelated fields, opening up new uses for underleveraged assets. Melinda Rolfs, an executive at Mastercard, which sells its anonymized transaction data and analytics to merchants and financial institutions, realized that the data could be made available free to charities and other nonprofits to bolster their fundraising efforts. She now spearheads Mastercard's data philanthropy program, creating value in new ways for the business and for society.

Experimentation: Test Smarter to Learn Faster

Experimentation is the process of turning a promising idea into a workable solution that addresses a real need. The big risk, once you start testing, is that confirmation biases and sunk cost effects will deaden your responsiveness to corrective feedback. Successful innovators design their experiments to learn faster and cheaper, and they remain open to sharp changes in direction. They test to *improve* rather than to *prove.*

The lean start-up methodology puts learning at the heart of its approach, and although that objective is certainly important, it often conflicts with the emphasis the model's proponents also put on speed. Frenetic cycles of build-measure-learn encourage organizations to settle for a "good enough" product-market fit, leading them to miss more-ambitious solutions.

Instead, externalize your idea early and often so that others can visualize, touch, or interact with it. When pitching his idea to doctors, Jorge Odón used a glass jar for a womb, a child's doll for a trapped baby, and a fabric bag sewn by his wife as his lifesaving device. This kind of low-cost mock-up is sometimes dubbed a Frankenstein prototype.

Negative reactions are as valuable as positive ones and are critical to avoiding costly errors. To take an extreme example, the pioneering architect Frank Gehry produces what he calls Shrek models, intended to make clients uncomfortable. ("Shrek" is Yiddish for "fear.") Successive models don't build on the ones before them; rather, they depict divergent approaches, enabling Gehry to explore and learn from client discomfort and allowing the ideas to mature.

Be careful not to overinvest in your prototype. The aim is to test without building. One way is to use off-the-shelf technology or human intervention to fake a functional product or service—a so-called Wizard of Oz prototype. Researchers working on robot-assisted therapy for health care interventions typically assess user reactions to proposed designs with a Wizard of Oz technique: Without the patient's knowledge, the "robot" is controlled by a human operator. This kind of mock-up lets the researchers explore their concepts before writing any code.

Digital tools are a great aid to simulation. A website or a video can create the illusion of an offering before it exists—as Dropbox did when it made a video demo of the prototype for its file-sharing software to avoid bringing to market a product no one would want.

Digital technology also simplifies A/B testing, whereby you propose two versions of an offering to learn what users value most. For example, the free, text-based service, Crisis Text Line, initially planned to use counselors from paid crisis centers on the hotline but pivoted after comparing their performance with that of volunteers trained in best practices that had been identified by digital text analysis. One salient finding from the analysis: "I" statements—discouraged in traditional counseling—were three times as effective as other statements in keeping discussions going. Armed with this type of knowledge, the volunteers outperformed their professional counterparts on every key indicator: They were faster and cheaper and got higher-quality ratings. This persuaded leadership to flip the business model, ditching the paid counselors in favor of trained volunteers.

Digital advances help you get closer to the ultimate goal in testing: trial without real-world error. To build his solar-powered plane, Bertrand Piccard approached conventional aircraft manufacturers, but they showed little interest. So he found partners outside the industry—80 in all. In conjunction with an advanced software and solutions provider, they created a "digital twin" of the plane, using 3D software to design and test the individual parts and complex assemblies. That allowed them to forgo costly and slow physical prototypes and simulate the plane's performance under a variety of conditions, dramatically reducing the number of dead ends. What started as a purely technological experiment became an experiment in virtual collaboration as well.

Navigation: Maneuver to Avoid Being Shot Down

To bring your idea to fruition, you'll need to adjust to the forces that can make or break it. But your belief in your idea—and your overfamiliarity with the context—may lead you to underestimate the effort needed to mobilize supporters and steer past obstacles. You must sharpen your reading of hostile environments, including your organization's own immune system, and meet multiple persuasion challenges. Original thinking is essential in shaping your business model as well as your offering.

The way an idea is framed affects how people perceive its value. Steve Sasson, the Kodak engineer who invented the digital camera, acknowledges that dubbing his innovation "filmless photography" was a serious hindrance to gaining internal support at a company whose very existence revolved around film. Your enthusiasm may blind you to the threat you pose to others, and your offering—often developed under the radar, with input only from trusted critics— may not survive first contact with skeptics.

By contrast, when Jonathan Ledgard conceived of drones as an answer to Africa's transport challenges, his adroit framing paved the way for acceptance: He called the unmanned aircraft "flying donkeys" (a reference to the loads they could carry), rendering a potentially menacing concept unthreatening, concrete, and sticky. An engaging frame uses the familiar to explain the less familiar and emphasizes continuity. If it resonates, digital channels can accelerate interest, as they did for Narayana Peesapaty's edible cutlery.

Presenting a disruptive innovation in a way that is responsive to the collective DNA of your organization is also crucial. According to Jean-Paul Bailly, who oversaw a dramatic transformation of the French National Mail Service (La Poste) from 2002 to 2013, "You have to demonstrate that the change can help you remain true to your identity." In 2010, even as the state-owned entity began to privatize, Bailly continued to emphasize public service values and public trust. Those core assets underpinned new activities, including e-commerce, banking, and mobile telephony. Building on public confidence in mail carriers, the organization added services for the elderly—an innovative response to both the country's aging population and the declining number of letters sent by post. Customers can now commission the local mail carrier to drop in on aging relatives, and postal workers are trained in the situations they might encounter when they do. Because of such measures, the transformation was completed without any layoffs, and the mail service's revenues have continually grown.

Even if you've managed to secure internal buy-in and user interest, remember that an entire ecosystem stands between you and those you hope to serve. The input, connections, or cooperation of an array of stakeholders could determine the outcome of your offering. Owlet devised a wireless wristband to monitor hospital patients' vital signs. The development team thought it had a winner, because neither patients nor nurses liked the wired products. But that issue was not a pain point for hospital administrators, who refused to pay for the wristbands. In focusing solely on users, Owlet had neglected buyers. It eventually hit the mark with a smart sock that tracks a sleeping infant's pulse and breathing and, when warranted, sends an alarm to the caregiver's smartphone. This time, crucially, the buyers—anxious parents—were also beneficiaries.

Successful navigation isn't just a matter of anticipating blockers; gaining support from unconventional allies can also be essential. The Mexico-born theme park KidZania is an indoor "city" where children can role-play adult jobs. When its founders ran out of development funds, they approached corporate sponsors—not just for financial support but also for professional expertise, facilitating a more realistic experience in terms of props, activities, architecture, and interiors. KidZania's industry partners create mini versions of their stores, banks, and offices, adding authenticity to the role-playing: Children can deliver packages dressed as DHL drivers or train to be pilots on a British Airways flight simulator. The concept took off, and KidZania became the world's fastest-growing group in experiential learning for children, with operations on five continents.

Digital technologies offer further opportunities for novel collaborations. For example, Vestergaard Frandsen (VF), a Switzerland-based disease-control company, devised an ingenious line of water filters, but they were too costly for the rural African and Indian communities that needed them most. Because the filters reduce emissions by eliminating the need to purify water over open fires, VF came up with the idea of distributing the devices free through funding from carbon offsets. To unlock that novel source of funding, it had to satisfy independent auditors that hundreds of thousands of filters were indeed being used. The platform's developers drew on an open-source data-collection platform developed at the

Further Reading

Attention

"Becoming a First-Class Noticer"
Max H. Bazerman
HBR, July–August 2014

Look: A Practical Guide for Improving Your Observational Skills
James H. Gilmore
Greenleaf Book Group, 2016

Perspective

"Are You Solving the Right Problems?"
Thomas Wedell-Wedellsborg
HBR, January–February 2017

The Pause Principle: Step Back to Lead Forward
Kevin Cashman
Berrett-Koehler, 2012

Imagination

"Find Innovation Where You Least Expect It"
Tony McCaffrey and Jim Pearson
HBR, December 2015

University of Washington to create a smartphone app that would let field representatives photograph recipients of the filters and record their homes' GPS coordinates. Thus each recipient was reachable for follow-up and auditing purposes—making the solution both scalable and sustainable.

A Flexible Sequence

For the sake of convenience, we've presented our framework as a kind of process. In practice, though, the five elements constitute not an orderly sequence or even a cycle but a mix that involves frequent crisscrossing among activities. This accounts for two realities that are often overlooked by conventional innovation methodologies:

The Dance of the Possible: The Mostly Honest Completely Irreverent Guide to Creativity
Scott Berkun
Berkun Media, 2017

Experimentation

"Increase Your Return on Failure"
Julian Birkinshaw and Martine Haas
HBR, May 2016

The Innovator's Hypothesis: How Cheap Experiments Are Worth More Than Good Ideas
Michael Schrage
MIT Press, 2014

Navigation

"How to Get Ecosystem Buy-In"
Martin Ihrig and Ian C. MacMillan
HBR, March–April 2017

The Obstacle Is the Way: The Timeless Art of Turning Trials into Triumph
Ryan Holiday
Portfolio, 2014

Multiple entry points

Although *attention* is a logical starting point for innovation, others are valid too. *Imagination* is a common gateway. Jorge Odón was not looking to improve on existing birthing equipment; the idea literally came to him in his sleep. Imagination was also the entry point for Bertrand Piccard's solar plane. His story shows that to achieve a breakthrough innovation, you don't necessarily have to know something no one else does; you can get there by believing in something no one else believes in. Design thinking has difficulty accommodating such big-leap innovation, which is based largely on a top-down belief in possibility rather than on present needs or technologies. Part of our genius as human beings is imagining that which is currently out of reach. Still-immature technology that might be available in a few years is not a direct focus of design-thinking methodologies.

Another entry point is *experimentation,* as when you stumble upon a finding that leads you not to merely pivot but to reboot. A few years ago Jeannette Garcia, a chemist at IBM Research who was seeking to synthesize a particular polymer, set up a chemical reaction and stepped away to fetch an ingredient. Returning to the flask, she found a bone-hard substance: It turned out she had discovered the first new class of polymers in decades. The new substance was superstrong, lightweight, and, unlike comparable materials, easily and infinitely recyclable. That unique combination makes it a breakthrough discovery with a wide range of potential applications in aerospace, autos, electronics, and 3D printing, although for now it remains a solution in search of meaningful problems.

Multiple pathways

Just as you can start anywhere in your creative process, you can proceed in any direction and switch focus as required. Existing innovation models do not explicitly acknowledge such freedom—and so they are often taken too literally and reduced to rigid, unrealistic recipes.

Consider Garcia's polymer discovery. Looking ahead, IBM has twin priorities to juggle: It must define relevant customer needs (attention) while deciding with whom it should partner (navigation) to bring a solution to fruition. This may involve much back-and-forth along with further experimentation (to produce prototypes) and occasionally stepping back (to maintain perspective and avoid overstretching).

The creative process is full of dead ends that may require you to revisit your original question, the options for responding, or your choice of partners (as CTL did when it pivoted away from established crisis professionals). Insights may occur after a partnership has been formed. Knowledge gained through experimentation may deepen your understanding of users and the problems they face. Sometimes you will address the challenge of asking the right people the right questions late in the process—as when Owlet realized that wireless health monitors were a pressing need not for hospital administrators but for new parents. Follow whatever sequence works for you. Process fixedness is itself a barrier to breakthrough innovations.

A caveat in closing: Although the order is flexible, you do need to touch all the elements at least once, because each one neutralizes different biases. Neglecting even one can lead you to focus on the wrong problem, idea, or solution. Creativity is a journey of sense making. By attending to all five elements, you will maximize your chances of reaching a truly game-changing innovation at the journey's end.

Originally published in November–December 2018. Reprint R1806H

Collaborating with Creative Peers

by Kimberly D. Elsbach, Brooke Brown-Saracino, and Francis J. Flynn

NOT LONG AGO, in the course of studying new product development, we were witnesses to a breakdown in the creative collaboration process. A toy company needed a hit offering for the next holiday shopping season. Early on, a marketer we'll call Kyle came to a meeting where one of the company's most talented game developers was previewing a car-and-racetrack game concept. During the discussion, Kyle piped up with his advice: "It needs some kind of creature." The developer paid little attention. If anything, he resented the feedback from someone who had no expertise in creative design.

But the marketer's intuition was sound. Several weeks later, the design team concluded that a villain (or "creature") would indeed make the game more engaging. Unfortunately, it was too late. Incorporating the new element would push the game's ship date beyond the holidays. So the whole project was shelved.

Our research into the dynamics of collaboration suggests that this scenario is fairly common. It can be difficult for people like Kyle—nonexperts with valuable input—to influence the work of creative colleagues. Small but significant numbers of these coworkers—whether they're innovative toy developers, clever advertising copywriters, brilliant biotech scientists, or whip-smart bank analysts—are generally much better at giving ideas than taking them.

In a recent set of studies, we decided to investigate why this phenomenon exists and what the Kyles of the world can do about it. We discovered that the problem centers not on ego but on identity. A healthy percentage of people in creative roles self-identify as "artists" and react in unproductive ways when they feel that identity is being threatened.

To be clear, we're not talking about *artistes* in the design department or accusing anyone of being thin-skinned; those are stereotypes that we'd actually like to erase. The people who think of themselves as artists work in a range of functions, and their passion for their work is often critical to the innovation and long-term success of their firms. But these artists differ from other creative people in an organization in that they feel a very personal stake in their endeavors. Their strength of feeling can energize them tremendously and sometimes drive them to achieve nothing short of genius. It may also make them resist useful feedback and great ideas if that input seems to put their core identity at risk.

So how can you work with these colleagues more effectively? The first step is to learn a little more about what makes your artistic peers tick. The second is to master four tactics that increase the odds of getting them to listen to—and incorporate—your ideas.

Understanding the Artist Identity

According to our studies, 15% to 20% of professionals in jobs that require creative work see themselves as "creators of unique outputs that embody personal, artistic visions." They prefer working independently on projects that they can "own" and that, in the end, will carry their distinctive stamp. This separates them from the majority of their creative peers, who typically self-identify as "problem solvers" and who readily embrace others' ideas, put their expertise into action in collaborative groups, and help channel projects toward commercial viability. In research on populations of toy designers, R&D scientists, and Hollywood screenwriters, we've found the mix of problem solvers and artists to be roughly the same.

Idea in Brief

Some people in creative roles seem immune to others' input. But this apparent arrogance is not actually what makes them tick. Their resistance may have less to do with size of ego than with sense of identity.

A subset of creative professionals identify as "artists," meaning they value three things: having a signature creative style so that their work bears a unique stamp; remaining involved in the execution of creative concepts rather than handing them off; and succeeding on noncommercial terms.

The authors suggest four tactics for working with artists:

1. **Offer broad suggestions.**

   - Artists may see specific, fully formed ideas as attempts to

wrest creative control. Plant just the seed of a concept, and you inspire continued engagement.

2. **Temper your enthusiasm.**

   - Don't act too invested in your own ideas. A dispassionate demeanor works better with artists.

3. **Delay decision making.**

   - Give artists ample time to consider your suggestions on their merits.

4. **Show respect and like-mindedness.**

   - Acknowledging an artist's prior thinking and work reassures him or her that your ideas are not off base.

Problem solvers are a known breed in most business contexts, but what does it mean to identify as an artist at work? In our interviews with many such professionals and their colleagues, three elements consistently surfaced.

A creative signature style

Artists feel pride in producing work that bears their unique stamp. As a result, some resist incorporating others' ideas into their projects, even when those suggestions address problems they'd like to solve. A common concern for artists, we find, is that the input might contaminate or dilute the special quality that marks the work as their own. One artistic toy designer admitted that she and people like her often react to proposed modifications with a reflexive "No. This is my idea. This is the way it should be." She explained, "A lot of times, if you're very idealistic and conceptual, you're not particularly open-minded."

Control over how ideas are executed

The artistic experts we interviewed weren't satisfied with simply launching a project; they wanted to see it through. One R&D scientist shared her frustration at being left out of decisions on packaging designs for a new candy she'd conceived. "We don't just add our two cents in part of the process," she said. "We actually create the whole thing." In short, artists want to control how their ideas are generated, shaped, and executed, not just contribute an initial design or vision.

Noncommercial motivation

Artists often see a fundamental antagonism between their own goals and those of their employers, causing them to resist influence from colleagues they perceive to be more profit-minded. One artistic toy designer put it this way: "The thing I would not want to do is give up who I am. If I become one of them [administrators], I lose all my value." He took pride in his constant "willingness to ignore rules, power, and authority." We saw this attitude bubble up especially in artists' interactions with marketing department colleagues, who were viewed as eager to strip concepts of the most innovative, interesting elements in order to widen their commercial appeal. "If somebody from marketing asks me to do it," another R&D scientist confessed, "my heart is not 100% in it."

Nonartists may misperceive these attitudes and behaviors as arrogance rather than as (at times unconscious) manifestations of creative identity. If they instead recognize why an artist colleague sometimes resists their ideas—and learn to offer input that doesn't feel like a violation of the person's signature expression, holistic control, and noncommercial ethos—productive collaboration becomes more likely.

Four Tactics for Advancing Your Ideas

Managers who want more give-and-take with their creative peers can use four proven tactics, identified by our research, that reduce threats to the artistic identity. (See the sidebar "Getting Traction When You Know You Have a Point.") These solutions are under-used, perhaps because they run counter to what is typically taught about collaboration and persuasion.

1. Offer broad suggestions

The researchers Susan Daniels-McGhee and Gary Davis have shown that specificity helps people visualize and build on proposed concepts, thereby facilitating collaboration. That makes sense in many settings. But when people are collaborating with artists, we find they are more likely to have influence when they avoid presenting specific ideas and, instead, offer broad suggestions or general inspiration.

For example, one executive at a large consumer-products company reported that when interacting with very creative people on her firm's R&D teams, she likes to offer "seed ideas." She said, "If you present [an idea] as not fully finished, people are more willing to think about it, take it into account, and then do something with [it]." By contrast, if you present a completely realized idea, you might imply that you're trying to impose your own creative stamp, take control of the process, or drive the project primarily from a commercial perspective. One artist we interviewed said that when people give him very specific suggestions, they seem "too focused on finishing the project rather than getting the idea right. It's almost like they've already decided on the way the project should go and have no respect for what I've done."

2. Temper your enthusiasm

Although artists believe passionately in their own ideas, they are more receptive to input from others when it is presented without emotion. Enthusiastic idea-givers can come off as keen on taking over the process, whereas people who are dispassionate seem less threatening. As one artistic R&D scientist put it, "Too much passion

Getting Traction When You Know You Have a Point

A MARKETING MANAGER we'll call Rhonda and a designer, Jim, worked at a food company that wanted to relaunch a popular product with new packaging. Jim presented a design concept involving an innovative material. Rhonda immediately noticed that it was unlikely to work in some environments—for example, in vending machines at gas stations, where fumes might penetrate the packaging and contaminate the product.

Her first impulse was to ask for a complete redesign, but recognizing that Jim was proud of his work, she held back. "If you think of it from his point of view, this is his baby," she explained. "He came up with the idea, and he designed the packaging from scratch. If you criticize it, he feels you're stopping his idea from going to market and reframing it into something else."

Instead, Rhonda used the tactics we describe in this article. She raised her concerns about the permeability of Jim's proposed material as an additional, interesting design challenge, not a flaw. "Look, we all want to see this happen," she was quick to say. "But we don't want to have a product that gets recalled." In a neutral, dispassionate tone of voice, she then pointed to some new trends in packaging that might provide general inspiration for getting around the problem. And she showed appreciation for Jim's expertise: "I said, 'I understand the merits of your idea because of A, B, and C. However, have you thought about D and E?' That showed him that I really did get what he was trying to do." She also made sure to ask questions and refer to the strengths of Jim's previous work.

Jim ultimately agreed to change the packaging, and the relaunch was successful—all thanks to a thoughtful approach of valuing Jim as an artist.

about their idea says to me, 'I don't need you anymore' and 'I'm going to do this my way.'" An artistic toy designer admitted that even when he seeks ideas from others, "there are [a] few people I might not ask because I know they are going to get overinvolved and take away my creative stamp on the project." This finding was particularly surprising to us, because in our own research on Hollywood pitch meetings, people were more effective at selling ideas when they expressed passion for them. But those are scenarios in which artists are seeking help from financial backers. When the artist is the audience, the approach must change.

3. Delay the decision making

It's best not to expect artists to react right away to an idea; instead, give them time to evaluate it on its merits. Your approach can be as simple as asking your colleague to "just think about it" or to "meet later to explore its potential." The delay gives artists not only more say over when and how to respond but also a chance to consider how they might incorporate your suggestion without detracting from their signature style. One manager at a food company described how she planned to suggest using a savory flavor in a conventionally sweet context to people on her firm's product design team: "If the idea blows their mind at first, it's really threatening to them. So it's better to ask them to go away and think about it a while . . . [so they can] see it might actually work with what they've already got going."

4. Show respect and like-mindedness

Our first three idea-giving tactics let artists retain some control so that, as one would-be collaborator put it, they "get their EQ out of the way and get their IQ thinking." The fourth tactic works from a different angle: It reassures creative colleagues that your ideas and theirs are likely to be congruent. Artists have told us that when someone shows familiarity with their existing ideas and previous work—and seems genuinely interested in learning about the creative process—the collaboration is more likely to be productive. You want to prove that you understand the artist's perspective and are on the same wavelength. This advice was explained well by a project manager who worked with an exacting food scientist; in fact, the scientist often referred to himself as the "czar" of his product. The project manager noticed that the best way to build mutual respect and become more "worthy" in the czar's eyes was to "be completely vulnerable," to show you'd made the effort to "get" his thinking, and to spend more time asking the right questions than presenting ideas. "Part of showing worthiness," he said, "is just asking."

We all know that creative collaborations typically yield better solutions than lone-genius efforts. But when you're not the creative expert in the room, it can be difficult to gain traction for your ideas. Our research reveals insights and practical strategies to increase your influence with your artist colleagues. It can also help managers enable all kinds of talent to flourish and create value together. By taking the time to understand how your colleagues' identities affect their perceptions and actions—and then behaving in ways that respect them—you reveal your own gifts as a collaborator and a professional.

Originally published in October 2015. Reprint R1510H

Creativity Under the Gun

by Teresa M. Amabile, Constance N. Hadley, and Steven J. Kramer

TRULY BREAKTHROUGH IDEAS rarely hatch overnight. Consider, for example, Charles Darwin's theory of evolution, which had a protracted evolution of its own. Darwin spent decades reading scientific literature, making voyages on the HMS *Beagle* to the Galápagos and other exotic destinations, carrying out painstakingly detailed observations, and producing thousands of pages of notes on those observations and his ideas for explaining them. It's inconceivable that his breakthrough would have occurred if he'd tried to rush it. In business, too, there are striking examples of the value of having relatively unstructured, unpressured time to create and develop new ideas. Scientists working at AT&T's legendary Bell Labs, operating under its corporate philosophy that big ideas take time, produced world-changing innovations including the transistor and the laser beam. Their ingenuity earned the researchers several Nobel prizes. They, like Darwin, had the time to think creatively.

But we can all point to examples where creativity seemed to be sparked by extreme time pressure. In 1970, during *Apollo* 13's flight to the moon, a crippling explosion occurred on board, damaging the air filtration system and leading to a dangerous buildup of carbon dioxide in the cabin. If the system could not be fixed or replaced, the astronauts would be dead within a few hours. Back at NASA mission control in Houston, virtually all engineers, scientists, and technicians immediately focused their attention on the problem. Working with a set of materials identical to those on board the spacecraft, they desperately tried to build a filtration system that the astronauts might be able to replicate. Every conceivable material was considered, including the cover of a flight procedure manual. With little time to spare, they came up with something that was ugly, inelegant, and far from perfect but that seemed like it just might do the job. The engineers quickly conveyed the design with enough clarity that the cognitively impaired astronauts were, almost unbelievably, able to build the filter. It worked, and three lives were saved.

The business examples of creativity under pressure are decidedly less dramatic than that, but they abound as well. The lauded design firm Ideo has put its innovative spin on personal computers, medical equipment, automotive electronics, toys, and even animatronic movie robots—and many of the new designs for those products were drawn up in three months or less. If you're like most managers, you have almost certainly worked with people who swear that they do their most creative work under tight deadlines. You may use pressure as a management technique, believing that it will spur people on to great leaps of insight. You may even manage yourself this way. If so, are you right?

Based on our research, the short answer is "no." When creativity is under the gun, it usually ends up getting killed. Although time pressure may drive people to work more and get more done, and may even make them *feel* more creative, it actually causes them, in general, to think less creatively. Of course, the short answer is not the whole story. Let's take a look at what time pressure is, how it feels when people experience it at work, and the different ways it can be managed to enhance creativity.

Fighting the Clock

Maria was a software developer on a team charged with creating an online system through which health care providers could access vital information about certain high-risk patients. It was critical that the new system be error-proof because the targeted patients were

Idea in Brief

Your most creative employees generate their best ideas under tight deadlines, right? Wrong. While time pressure may make people *feel* more creative, it usually prevents them from actually *thinking* creatively—juggling new ideas until they collide in original and ultimately profitable ways. When creativity is under the gun, it usually gets killed.

What's a manager to do? Your company's ability to develop the products and services of tomorrow depends on the highest levels of creativity. But time pressure and distractions usually rule. On highest-pressure days, most people are 45% *less* likely to think creatively than on lower-pressure days.

Still, in some organizations, creativity thrives *despite* brutal deadlines. How? Managers minimize time pressure's toll and use it to inspire fresh thinking. They enable people to stay immersed in important work—without interruption. And they make it crystal clear that the urgency is legitimate.

elderly or severely disabled individuals; in life-threatening situations, accurate information about them had to be communicated instantly. Unfortunately, the original contract for the project had vastly underestimated the time required to develop it. As a result, Maria and her team found themselves under extreme time pressure as the deadline approached. (Maria's identity, like all individual, project, and corporate identities in this article, has been disguised.)

The team was working almost around the clock, even though it was becoming clearer with each passing day that the complex technical problems it encountered simply could not be solved adequately within the original time frame. Yet senior management, as well as the project leader, pressed the team to meet the deadline, no matter what. Maria recorded her experiences during this time in a daily diary:

"At 7:30 this morning, my team leader asked me what my game plan was for the day and if I could be available for a rollout meeting. I wrote out on a flip chart what I thought needed to be done today, looked at the list, and told him it was two or three days of work. Now, as I am burned out and preparing to leave for the day, I look at the flip chart and realize that, at best, 20% of the work has been accomplished. This one-day list is really a four- or five-day list. The thing that most

Idea in Practice

Protecting Creativity

Creativity can flourish or fade under all kinds of time pressure. Here's what makes the difference:

On a mission: High-pressure, creative days are filled with focus and meaningful urgency. People concentrate on one project for most of the day, feel engaged in their work, and understand why their project is crucial. If they're collaborating, it's usually one-on-one.

On a treadmill: On high-pressure, low-creativity days, people feel they're running faster but getting further behind. Pulled in multiple directions, they feel unfocused, confused, and trapped in group meetings.

On an expedition: Low-pressure days yield creativity when people focus more on exploring ideas than on simply identifying problems, and when they collaborate one-on-one rather than in groups.

On autopilot: Low-pressure days generate no creativity when people do their jobs without engaging. Managers provide little encouragement to think in fresh ways, and employees languish in numerous meetings.

Catalyzing Creativity Under Pressure

To help employees feel they're on a mission or an expedition, rather than on a treadmill or autopilot:

- **Resist the illusion that pressure spurs creativity.** It usually doesn't. At AT&T's Bell Labs, the philosophy that "big ideas take time" sparked revolutionary

sticks in my mind from the entire day is that blasted flip chart with so little crossed off."

A few days later, Maria seemed even closer to the end of her rope:

"I told my supervisor that the hours I am working are completely unacceptable and that I planned to leave the company if this continued to be the norm on projects here. The look on his face was a bit aghast. Was he really shocked? Could this possibly be a surprise? All afternoon I felt physically drained, as if I were running on low blood sugar. I slept very poorly last night, several hours awake in the middle of the night. I feel physically exhausted again right now—lack of mental clarity, lack of motivation about the project."

Maria wasn't alone in her sense of the extreme time pressure the group was working under. Richard, another member of the team, kept his own diary during this period and had this to say:

innovations—the transistor, the laser beam—earning researchers seven Nobel prizes.

- **On low-pressure days, encourage people to play with ideas and develop something new.** 3M famously encourages scientists to devote 15% of their workweeks to creative endeavors—even those far afield from their assigned work.

- **Articulate realistic goals.** To stimulate the creative insights that send a project leapfrogging ahead to exciting solutions, design feasible project plans that reflect real requirements for success.

- **Protect time-pressured creative thinkers from distractions and unrelated demands.** In one study, engineers who gave one another uninterrupted quiet time during specified periods of every day accomplished more and felt better about their work.

- **Explain why tight deadlines are necessary.** Employees feel a sense of mission when they understand the urgent need for their work. They feel they're on a treadmill if they suspect you've handed down arbitrary deadlines just to get them running faster.

- **Encourage one-on-one collaboration.** Too many obligatory group meetings spawn feelings of fragmentation and wasted time.

- **Minimize abrupt scheduling changes.** You'll reduce uncertainty, helping people concentrate on their real work.

"The team leader announced that the project's core hours—when everyone is expected to be in the office and working—have been extended: 'They are now 8 a.m. to 7 p.m., and don't make social plans for the next three weekends, as we will likely be working.' This project is now officially a death march in my mind. I can't fathom how much work we have left, how severely we underestimated this project, and how complex this dog has become. At every turn, we uncover more things that are unsettled, incomplete, or way more complex than we ever thought."

We collected more than 9,000 such diary entries in a recent study of 177 employees in seven U.S. companies. Our objective was to look deeply at how people experienced time pressure day to day as they worked on projects that required high levels of inventiveness, while also measuring their ability to think creatively under such pressure.

Trapping Creativity in the Wild

MANY OF THE FINDINGS we report in this article are drawn from a study of time pressure and creativity that we recently conducted with Jennifer Mueller of Yale School of Management and William Simpson and Lee Fleming, both of Harvard Business School. That study included data from 177 employees who were members of 22 project teams from seven U.S. companies within three industries (chemical, high tech, and consumer products). More than 85% of the participants had college degrees, and many had graduate education. In order to be included in the study, a team had to be identified by senior management as working on a project where creativity was both possible and desirable. In other words, these projects, and our participants, were considered the "creative lifeblood" of their organizations. We believed that we could better understand what these people were experiencing each day, and what was really influencing their creativity, if we tracked what was happening in real time.

To accomplish this, we emailed each member of each team a brief daily questionnaire throughout the entire course of their projects. We asked them to fill it out and return it to us at the end of each workday. Somewhat amazingly, 75% of the questionnaires that we sent out were returned completed even though some of the projects we followed lasted more than six months. This yielded the very high number of returns (9,134) that we analyzed in this study. The questionnaires contained several numerical-scale items about the work and the work environment, including one that asked participants to rate the day's time pressure on a seven-point scale. A similar item asked them to rate the creativity of their work that day.

The most interesting part of the questionnaire was the narrative diary entry, in which we asked participants to briefly describe one event that stood out in their minds from the day—anything at all that related to the project, the team, or their work. (We did not ask them to focus on creativity.) Because we asked for just one standout event each day, the diaries do not present a comprehensive account of everything that happened that day. We assume, though, that they are a representative sample of the important things that were happening. And although we saw some clear patterns in the results, further research will be necessary to determine definitively what is causing what.

Specifically, we asked each of the participants—most of whom were highly educated knowledge workers—to complete a diary form online in which they rated several aspects of their work and their work environment that day, including how much time pressure they felt. In a separate section of the form, we also asked them to describe

The diary entries provided rich information about what people were doing and experiencing each day. We derived a "creative thinking" measure by coding each diary narrative. A narrative was considered to have evidence of creative thinking if it described an event in which the person was engaged in any form of creative thinking as the term is used in everyday language; this included mentions of discovery, brainstorming, generating ideas, thinking flexibly, or "being creative." We also included many of the cognitive processes that theorists believe are important in facilitating creative thinking: learning, insight, realization, awareness, clarification, remembering, and focused concentration. All of these processes are included in what we call "creative thinking," "thinking creatively," or "creativity" in this article. (For more details on the methods and findings of our research, see the working paper by Teresa M. Amabile, Jennifer M. Mueller, William B. Simpson, Constance N. Hadley, Steven J. Kramer, and Lee Fleming, "Time Pressure and Creativity in Organizations: A Longitudinal Field Study," HBS, 2002.)

In preparing this article, we went beyond the statistical analyses of the time-pressure study to develop a richer view of the conditions under which time pressure may or may not have negative effects. For that purpose, we looked at four extreme conditions: days of very high time pressure when creative thinking did happen; days of very high time pressure when creative thinking didn't happen; days of very low time pressure when creative thinking did happen; and days of very low time pressure when creative thinking didn't happen. We took a sample of 100 diary entries from each of these four work conditions and read them carefully to discern patterns that distinguished them from one another—for instance, that creativity seemed more likely when people were able to focus on a single activity for most of the day.

In addition to that qualitative analysis, we used the numerical ratings that the participants reported in the questionnaires to examine the number of hours they worked; the degree of challenge, involvement, and time pressure they felt; the number of people they worked with; and the degree of distraction they felt. The results of our analyses are summarized in the exhibit "The time-pressure/creativity matrix."

something that stood out in their minds about that day, and we carefully analyzed those short entries for evidence of creative thinking. (See the sidebar "Trapping Creativity in the Wild" for a detailed description of our research method, including our study's specific definition of "creative thinking.")

What we saw in those diary entries was both fascinating and sobering. Many of the people in our study reported experiences similar to Maria's: They often felt overworked, fragmented, and burned out. At the most basic level, then, we found support for recent observations in the popular press that Americans are feeling a time crunch at work, creating what one *Newsweek* reporter called a nation of "the quick, or the dead-tired." The problem has been with us for some time. As early as 1995, *U.S. News & World Report* described a nationwide poll showing that more than half of Americans wanted more free time, even if it meant earning less money. And in 1996, according to a *Wall Street Journal–NBC News* survey, 75% of those people earning more than $100,000 a year cited managing their time as a bigger problem than managing their money.

Time pressure has become a fact of life for the American worker. On the average day, our study participants reported feeling "moderate" time pressure—and that was the average. A great many of the participants' workdays were characterized by "extremely" high levels of time pressure. "Today I realized that our time to get ready for the upcoming presentations was almost nonexistent," wrote one participant in a fairly typical entry. Another, in a different company, lamented, "Overnight, I had to come up with a fully detailed plan for the remainder of the development phase, to let us know how far behind we were."

Perhaps not surprisingly, although our participants said time pressure was rather high most of the time, we noticed a trend whereby time pressure seemed to build as work projects went from early to later stages; as with Maria's project, people felt more and more pressed for time as deadlines approached. Interestingly, we also observed a slight trend in time-pressure changes during the week: The time pressure started out relatively low on Mondays, increased through the week to a peak on Thursdays, and decreased on Fridays. This may be because managers' expectations for productivity are somewhat lower on Mondays and Fridays. Or perhaps it's simply that, on the days bracketing the weekend, people are already (or still) in a weekend mindset and less subject to feeling the time pressure that exists. We also found that people were more likely to report high levels of time pressure on days when they were traveling for work or working off-site. It's possible that people try to pack more work into such days to minimize the total time spent away from the office. And, of course, the many hassles of travel itself undoubtedly contribute to feelings of being pressed.

Energy and Frustration

As described in the diaries, the days when our study participants felt extreme time pressure were noticeably different from the days when they felt less time pressure. People tended to work more hours and were involved in a greater number of activities, having to switch gears more often, on time-pressured days. That provides us with our first clue about how time pressure might affect creativity—a clue to which we will return later.

People experienced different feelings as time pressure increased, but we can't simply say that they felt better or worse. It was a mixed bag. At first, people felt more involved in and challenged by their work: "I am under a lot of pressure to start up the manufacturing machine for our new product this week . . . I was actually happy to run to the hardware stores for hose fittings and bolts. For the first time, I feel like we are truly making real progress." And, in surprising contrast to Maria's reaction of feeling drained, people generally felt more energized under high pressure. As one diarist reported, "We are three-quarters of the way there! I really enjoy seeing the team pull together."

But some people also experienced deep frustration as time pressure increased: "I frequently feel I am swimming upstream on this project and always buried with work." In particular, they seemed frustrated by constant distractions from other team members on time-pressured days. One of our study participants told a particularly vivid story about his frustration with a colleague:

"We had a meeting about what is going wrong with the filtration program and how to come to an acceptable level of understanding and information gathering. As usual, Paul, Emilio, Sarah, and I were going at breakneck speed trying to make sure we're all pulling together. But Raj could only repeatedly say, 'But what part of my job don't you want me to do, if you expect me to do that?' He was argumentative and negative, and all I could think was, 'Stop it!' I was able to control myself and didn't scream at him, but I was close."

When we look at the whole picture of how people were experiencing time pressure, it seems they were working hard, spending long hours on the job, and sometimes feeling jazzed about what they were doing. But at the same time, there was a lot of frustration—another clue that will help us understand time pressure's effects on creativity.

The Pressure Trap

Our study indicates that the more time pressure people feel on a given day, the less likely they will be to think creatively. Surprisingly, though, people seem to be largely unaware of this phenomenon. In their assessments of their own creativity each day, the participants in our study generally perceived themselves as having been *more* creative when time pressure was high. Sadly, their diaries gave the lie to those self-assessments. There was clearly less and less creative thinking in evidence as time pressure increased.

Moreover, the drop in creative thinking was most apparent when time pressure was at its worst. In the daily diary form, participants were asked to rate the time pressure they felt on a scale of one to seven, with seven being the highest level of pressure. On the days rated a seven, people were 45% less likely to think creatively than they were on any of the lower-pressure days.

Managers might think that the occasional uncreative day is simply the price paid for keeping work on a highly productive schedule. If your creative juices freeze up on a particularly busy Thursday, they might argue, you'll be able to get back to creativity on Friday when the demands have died down a bit. But maybe not. To our surprise, more time pressure on a certain day meant less creative thinking that day, the next day, *and* the day after that. In other words, whether because of exhaustion or enduring postpressure cognitive paralysis, our study participants seemed to experience a "pressure hangover" that lasted a couple of days at least.

That lingering time-pressure effect showed up whether we examined time pressure day to day or over longer periods. The higher the overall sense of time pressure that participants felt during the first week of their projects, the lower the level of creative thinking we saw from them during the first half of their projects (a period that varied from three weeks to four months). And the higher the overall sense of time pressure at the midpoint, the lower the level of creative thinking in the second half.

Why does time pressure have this dampening effect on creativity? Psychological research over the past 30 years, along with theories about how creativity happens, can help to explain. Psychologists have long believed that creativity results from the formation of a large number of associations in the mind, followed by the selection of associations that may be particularly interesting and useful. In a sense, it's as if the mind is throwing a bunch of balls into the cognitive space, juggling them around until they collide in interesting ways. The process has a certain playful quality to it; in fact, Einstein once referred to creativity as "combinatorial play." If associations are made between concepts that are rarely combined—that is, if balls that don't normally come near one another collide—the ultimate novelty of the solution will be greater.

Considerable research, drawn from experiments and from observations of creative activities, supports this view of the creative process. And some recent research suggests that the success of the combinatorial process depends both on having sufficient time to create the balls to juggle—exploring concepts and learning things that might somehow be useful—and having sufficient time to devote to the actual juggling. For example, one study we and our colleagues conducted found that people who allocate more time to exploratory behaviors while doing a task produce work that is rated by experts as more creative. Another study found that simply having a few minutes to think through a task—studying the materials, playing around with them—can lead to more creativity than having to dive into the task cold. So we have still more clues about how being under the gun might affect the creative process.

A Peek into the Diaries

THESE DIARY EXCERPTS were written by study participants who experienced the four work conditions described in this article. See if you or your employees might say something similar about experiences in your own organization.

On a Mission
(High Time Pressure, High Likelihood of Creative Thinking)

"At the end of the day today, after getting the documents ready, it hit me as to how creative Katherine and I had been together when we had worked in a room, away from the telephones, noise, interruptions, and other distractions. I felt very satisfied with the work we produced."

"Just as I was knee-deep in 1s and 0s, staring at an execution trace of the firmware (which was acting strangely), I got three phone calls in a row. I was about ready to throw the damn phone across the room. Fortunately, it stopped ringing after that, and I was able to refocus and find the problem. Hooray."

"We found out today that the drop test on one of our products was not done properly, and we needed a way to pad our product in a rush. I remembered that we had $10 million worth of an obsolete cell cushion that we were getting ready to write off, and I suggested we use that. It worked great!"

"I brought in some of my personal camera equipment today and used it to create a high-magnification video analysis system . . . I felt this was very creative work on my part—passing on my knowledge of optics and photography to an engineer who will continue with this work."

On an Expedition
(Low Time Pressure, High Likelihood of Creative Thinking)

"In my meeting with Seth to discuss the imaging model, several ideas he mentioned meshed with ideas I had, and I came away with a better and more detailed model."

"Wendy brought in her samples of the ILP films and presented them to me in a way that really made sense and triggered a lot of good ideas on my end."

"John spent time discussing promotional opportunities with me, and I felt like I was really learning something."

"I tried out my patterned adhesive wine labels in the lab. Bought wine at the grocery store and committed sacrilege by pouring it into the sink. My patterned adhesive didn't really work well, but I made some interesting ob-servations that helped me understand the problem a little better."

"While brainstorming ideas for solving the axle retention problem, I discov-ered a way to reduce the cost of our current wheeled container. In addition, this may give us a better product that is easier to produce. I made a few calls to begin investigating the feasibility."

On a Treadmill
(High Time Pressure, Low Likelihood of Creative Thinking)

"I spent the day trying to get a business plan finished—or at least started—for this strategic alliance. I was very frustrated by constant interruptions, which make it necessary to get this type of work done before or after hours."

"Today was a very long day spent in several meetings. We spend so much time covering old issues instead of driving the business forward."

"I was informed that I have to come up with a new launch rationale by Monday so it can be reviewed by the operating team. The relaunching of the old print-ers is devoid of any logical strategy. Now I have to make up one that sounds good."

"One problem after another occurred today. I had intended to complete several different items for the product transfer, but I spent the day fighting fires instead."

On Autopilot
(Low Time Pressure, Low Likelihood of Creative Thinking)

"Very low energy today. Must be the weather, but I feel whipped. Focused on organizing and planning. Put out an agenda for the optimization meeting tomorrow."

"Overall feeling of depression today."

"Mostly just doing paperwork. I cleaned up a lot of outstanding items."

"The team had an all-day meeting with the general manager. He just raised three questions, rather than giving us a clear leadership response to what we've done."

"Today I gave a two-hour presentation on product strategy and plans for the new product launch to our European marketing managers. I was disap-pointed by their [apathetic] response. The same old issues came up and a moderately negative attitude prevailed."

Protecting Creativity

Even though time pressure seems to undermine creative thinking in general, there are striking exceptions. We know, from our own study and from anecdotal evidence, that people can and do come up with ingenious solutions under desperately short time frames. What makes the difference? It's time to put the clues together.

When we compared the diary entries from the time-pressured days when creative thinking happened to the entries from the time-pressured days when no creative thinking happened, we found that the creative days featured a particular—and rather rare—set of working conditions. Above all else, these days were marked by a sense of focus. People were able to concentrate on a single work activity for a significant portion of the day. As one diarist jubilantly declared: "The event of the day was that I had no standout events. I was able to concentrate on the project at hand without interruptions." This focus was often hard-won, as the individuals or their managers went to great lengths to protect their work from interruptions and other disturbances: "There were so many interruptions for chitchat that I couldn't get any decent work accomplished. I eventually had to go work very quietly in another room to get some of it done."

Indeed, this sense of focus implies some degree of isolation. On the time-pressured days that still yielded creative thinking, we noted that collaboration was limited. When it happened, it was somewhat more likely to be done in a concentrated way—for instance, working with another individual rather than in a group: "I had a chance to talk at the end of the day with Susan. She helped confirm that the path I was taking was right and helped me figure out some of the differences in the codes. Her help will keep me going."

Another key condition for achieving creativity on the high-pressure days was interpreting the time pressure as meaningful urgency. People understood why solving a problem or completing a job was crucial, and they bought into that urgency, feeling as though they were *on a mission*. (See the exhibit "The time-pressure/creativity matrix" for a summary of the work conditions

The time-pressure/creativity matrix

Our study suggests that time pressure affects creativity in different ways depending on whether the environment allows people to focus on their work, conveys a sense of meaningful urgency about the tasks at hand, or stimulates or undermines creative thinking in other ways.

	Time pressure	
	Low	High
High	Creative thinking under low time pressure is more likely when people feel as if they are **on an expedition**. They: • Show creative thinking that is more oriented toward generating or exploring ideas than identifying problems • Tend to collaborate with one person rather than with a group	Creative thinking under extreme time pressure is more likely when people feel as if they are **on a mission**. They: • Can focus on one activity for a significant part of the day because they are undistracted or protected • Believe that they are doing important work and report feeling positively challenged by and involved in the work • Show creative thinking that is equally oriented toward identifying problems and generating or exploring ideas
Likelihood of creative thinking		
Low	Creative thinking under low time pressure is unlikely when people feel as if they are **on autopilot**. They: • Receive little encouragement from senior management to be creative • Tend to have more meetings and discussions with groups rather than with individuals • Engage in less collaborative work overall	Creative thinking under extreme time pressure is unlikely when people feel as if they are **on a treadmill**. They: • Feel distracted • Experience a highly fragmented workday, with many different activities • Don't get the sense that the work they are doing is important • Feel more pressed for time than when they are "on a mission" even though they work the same number of hours • Tend to have more meetings and discussions with groups rather than with individuals • Experience lots of last-minute changes in their plans and schedules

our study participants experienced.) They were involved in their work and felt positively challenged by it. The sense of urgency and the ability to focus are probably related, for two reasons. If people believe that their work is vitally important, they may be more willing and able to ignore a variety of distractions in their workdays. Meanwhile, managers who share this sense of urgency may free people from less essential tasks. This was clearly the case in the *Apollo* 13 mission: All nonessential work was abandoned until the air filtration problem was solved and the astronauts were returned home safely.

But when this protected focus was missing on time-pressured days—and it very often was—people felt more like they were *on a treadmill.* On these days, our diarists reported a more extreme level of time pressure even though they were not working more hours, and they felt much more distracted. When recording the number of different activities they performed, they were likely to use words like "several," "many," and "too numerous to count." They were pulled in too many directions, unable to focus on a single activity for any significant period of time. One diarist, paraphrasing the oft-repeated lament, said: "The faster I run, the behinder I get."

Our first clue, that people might have to switch gears more often under time pressure, underlies this treadmill condition; many things are clamoring for people's attention simultaneously. Remember, too, our clue that feelings of time pressure are associated with frustration, especially frustration with other members of a team. We suspect that interruptions contribute to that frustration. Other evidence adds to the picture of a distracted, disturbed, confusing environment on treadmill days. People had many more meetings and discussions with groups rather than with individuals. Moreover, they often had to cope with last-minute changes to schedules and plans. In many ways, they seemed to be operating under greater uncertainty: "At the meeting, we discovered that the work we have done to date may have to be completely redone because of a decision made by upper management to change the way the new system will process customer orders." On these low-focus, time-pressured days, people weren't very likely to see what they were doing as important or to feel a meaningful sense of urgency to complete a project or task.

Did an absence of time pressure guarantee that people would be more creative? Certainly not. Under any level of time pressure, low or high, reports of creative thinking were relatively rare; they showed up in only about 5% of the 9,000-plus daily diary reports. Under low time pressure, the differences in whether creativity happened or not seem to lie in the way people were spending their days. Most noticeably, when people exhibited creativity in the absence of time pressure, they were more oriented toward exploring and generating new ideas than identifying problems to be solved. (Remember our clue from the psychological literature on combinatorial play.) People behaved as if they were *on an expedition*. In addition, if people in this condition worked with someone else, they tended to spend the day (or part of it) collaborating with only one other person; collaboration with many people was rare. Having a single focal point to bounce new ideas off of might help people stay oriented toward the work on these more relaxed days, in contrast to having many "playmates" at once.

Finally, of course, there were days when people didn't feel under much time pressure and didn't show any evidence of creative thinking. They seemed to be doing their jobs, putting one foot in front of the other, without engaging too deeply in what was happening. They behaved as though they were *on autopilot*. On these days, there was a generally low level of collaborative work, although there were more meetings and discussions that involved groups rather than individuals. And people felt the least encouragement from high-level management to do creative work. Perhaps if creativity had been encouraged more, these individuals would have made better use of their relatively low-pressure days.

Lessons for Management—and Self-Management

Our research focused on knowledge workers—people who, according to researcher Leslie Perlow, are most likely to suffer from a "time famine" in contemporary American organizations. These are the people from whom we need and expect the highest levels of creativity; they are developing the products, services, and organizations of tomorrow. They are also the people who are most handicapped in their quest to be creative.

There's no doubt that creative thinking is possible under high—even extreme—time pressure. But this seems to be likely only in a situation that, research suggests, is not the norm in modern organizations: being able to become deeply immersed, and stay deeply immersed, in an important, urgent problem. Given the demands in most organizations for communication and process checks, as well as the prevalence of highly interdependent work roles, protected creativity time does not occur naturally. What, then, can managers do to minimize the negative effects of time pressure and use it appropriately in the service of creativity? What can each of us do to maintain our own creativity in today's pressured organizations?

Our first suggestion is the obvious one: Avoid extreme time pressure whenever possible, particularly if you are looking for high levels of learning, exploration, idea generation, and experimentation with new concepts. Don't be fooled into thinking that time pressure will, in itself, spur creativity. That's a powerful illusion but an illusion nonetheless. Complex cognitive processing takes time, and, without some reasonable time for that processing, creativity is almost impossible.

Of course, it would be foolish to think that the ideal for creativity is a complete absence of time pressure on a particular work project. Given the demands that modern life puts on people, it's too likely that other things would steal attention from the project—the urgent would drive out the important—and nothing would be accomplished. Moreover, it would be easy for people to slip into autopilot mode if there were no sense of urgency. Our research suggests that low time pressure doesn't necessarily foster creative thinking—but that it can do so when people are encouraged to learn, to play with ideas, and to develop something truly new. Consider the creativity-shielding practices at 3M. For many years, that innovation powerhouse has had a tradition of protecting 15% of the workweek for creative endeavors. All its R&D scientists devote that time to exploring whatever new ideas or pet projects most intrigue them personally, even if those ideas and projects are far afield from their assigned work.

For most companies, the best way to avoid undue time pressure is to articulate goals at all levels of the organization that are realistic and carefully planned, avoiding the optimism bias that plagues a lot of corporate planning. Announcing that a certain number of new products will be developed in the coming year, without a sense of the feasibility of that goal, will probably cause extreme time pressure to ripple through the organization—right down to the people who are actually supposed to be coming up with the ideas for those products. Signing a contract that promises to deliver items to a client by a certain date, without careful scoping of what the project will likely involve, can lead to the treadmill mentality that we saw on Maria's team. People may continue to advance the work, but they won't have the creative insights that will send the project leapfrogging ahead to truly exciting solutions.

In situations where time pressure can't be avoided, managers should focus on protecting time-pressured people who are supposed to be doing creative work from interruptions, distractions, and unrelated demands for a significant portion of each workweek. This concentration on "real work" can reduce the time fragmentation that we saw in so many of our participants' daily diaries.

Perlow's research in a high-tech firm, as reported in her book *Finding Time: How Corporations, Individuals, and Families Can Benefit from New Work Practices* (Cornell University Press, 1997), showed that engineers who agreed to give one another such uninterrupted quiet time during specified periods each day were able to get more done on their projects and felt better about their workdays. Her research also suggested, unfortunately, that it is difficult to sustain such a major change in workday norms without deep cultural change in the organization.

Creativity can also be supported under time-pressured conditions if managers can help people understand why tight time frames are necessary. It's much easier to feel that you are on a mission if you accept that there is an important, urgent need for the work you are doing, rather than feeling that an arbitrary deadline has been handed down simply to make you run ever faster on your treadmill. Our research suggests that managers should also encourage one-on-one collaborations and discussions, avoiding an excess of the obligatory group meetings that may contribute to feelings of fragmentation and wasted time. Finally, people may be better able to concentrate on their work if managers minimize abrupt changes in scheduled activities and plans.

In short, the key to protecting creative activity—including your own—is to offset the effects of extreme time pressure. The obvious way to do that is to reduce the time pressure. But in cases where it is unavoidable, its negative effects can be softened somewhat by getting your people and yourself in the mindset of being on a mission—sharing a sense that the work is vital and the urgency legitimate. It also means ruthlessly guarding protected blocks of the workweek, shielding staff from the distractions and interruptions that are the normal condition of organizational life. The best situation for creativity is not to be under the gun. But if you can't manage that, at least learn to dodge the bullets.

Originally published in August 2002. Reprint R0208C

Strategy Needs Creativity

by Adam Brandenburger

I'VE NOTICED THAT BUSINESS SCHOOL STUDENTS often feel frustrated when they're taught strategy. There's a gap between what they learn and what they'd like to learn. Strategy professors (including me) typically teach students to think about strategy problems by introducing them to rigorous analytical tools—assessing the five forces, drawing a value net, plotting competitive positions. The students know that the tools are essential, and they dutifully learn how to use them. But they also realize that the tools are better suited to understanding an existing business context than to dreaming up ways to reshape it. Game-changing strategies, they know, are born of creative thinking: a spark of intuition, a connection between different ways of thinking, a leap into the unexpected.

They're right to feel this way—which is not to say that we should abandon the many powerful analytical tools we've developed over the years. We'll always need them to understand competitive landscapes and to assess how companies can best deploy their resources and competencies there. But we who devote our professional lives to thinking about strategy need to acknowledge that just giving people those tools will not help them break with conventional ways of thinking. If we want to teach students—and executives—how to generate groundbreaking strategies, we must give them tools explicitly designed to foster creativity.

A number of such tools already exist, often in practitioner-friendly forms. In "How Strategists Really Think: Tapping the Power of Analogy" (HBR, April 2005), Giovanni Gavetti and Jan W. Rivkin write compellingly about using analogies to come up with new business models. Charles Duhigg talks in his book *Smarter Faster Better* about introducing carefully chosen creative "disturbances" into work processes to spur new thinking. Youngme Moon, in "Break Free from the Product Life Cycle" (HBR, May 2005), suggests redefining products by boldly limiting—rather than augmenting—the features offered.

What these approaches have in common is the goal of moving strategy past the insights delivered by analytic tools (which are close at hand) and into territory that's further afield, or—to use a bit of academic jargon—*cognitively distant.* They take their inspiration more from how our thought processes work than from how industries or business models are structured. For that reason they can help strategists make the creative leap beyond what already exists to invent a genuinely new way of doing business. Simply waiting for inspiration to strike is not the answer.

In this article I explore four approaches to building a breakthrough strategy:

- **Contrast.** The strategist should identify—and challenge—the assumptions undergirding the company's or the industry's status quo. This is the most direct and often the most powerful way to reinvent a business.

- **Combination.** Steve Jobs famously said that creativity is "just connecting things"; many smart business moves come from linking products or services that seem independent from or even in tension with one another.

- **Constraint.** A good strategist looks at an organization's limitations and considers how they might actually become strengths.

- **Context.** If you reflect on how a problem similar to yours was solved in an entirely different context, surprising insights

Idea in Brief

The Problem

The field of strategy overfocuses on analytic rigor and underfocuses on creativity.

Why It Matters

Analytic tools are good at helping strategists develop business ideas that are close at hand—but less

good at discovering transformative strategies.

In Practice

The wise strategist can work with four creativity-enhancing tools: contrast, combination, constraint, and context.

---

may emerge. (I wrote about these ideas more academically in "Where Do Great Strategies Really Come From?" *Strategy Science,* December 2017.)

These approaches aren't exhaustive—or even entirely distinct from one another—but I've found that they help people explore a wide range of possibilities.

Contrast: What Pieces of Conventional Wisdom Are Ripe for Contradiction?

To create a strategy built on contrast, first identify the assumptions implicit in existing strategies. Elon Musk seems to have a knack for this approach. He and the other creators of PayPal took a widely held but untested assumption about banking—that transferring money online was feasible and safe between institutions but not between individuals—and disproved it. With SpaceX he is attempting to overturn major assumptions about space travel: that it must occur on a fixed schedule, be paid for by the public, and use onetime rockets. He may be on track toward a privately funded, on-demand business that reuses rockets.

It's best to be precise—even literal—when naming such assumptions. Consider the video rental industry in 2000. Blockbuster ruled the industry, and the assumptions beneath its model seemed self-evident: People pick up videos at a retail location close to home. Inventory must be limited because new videos are expensive. Since the demand for them is high, customers must be charged for late returns. (It was basically a public-library model.) But Netflix put those assumptions under a microscope. Why is a physical location necessary? Mailing out videos would be cheaper and more convenient. Is there a way around the high fees for new releases? If the studios were open to a revenue-sharing agreement, both parties could benefit. Those two changes allowed Netflix to carry lots more movies, offer long rental periods, do away with late fees—and remake an industry.

Most of the time, strategy from contrast may look less revolutionary than Netflix (which remade itself again by streaming videos and becoming a content creator) or SpaceX (should it succeed). Any organization can ask whether it might usefully flip the order in which it performs activities, for example. The traditional model in retail is to start with a flagship store (usually in a city center) and add satellites (in suburban locations). Now consider pop-up stores: In some cases they conform to the old model—they are like mini-satellites; but in others the pop-up comes first, and if that's successful, a larger footprint is added. The Soho area of New York City has become a testing ground for this strategy.

Another approach is to consider shaking up the value chain, which in any industry is conventionally oriented in a particular way, with some players acting as suppliers and others as customers. Inverting the value chain may yield new business models. In the charitable sector, for example, donors have been seen as suppliers of financial resources. DonorsChoose.org is a model that treats them more like customers. The organization puts up a "storefront" of requests posted by schoolteachers around the United States who are looking for materials for their (often underresourced) classrooms. Donors can choose which requests to respond to and receive photos of the schoolwork that their money has supported. In effect, they are buying the satisfaction of seeing a particular classroom before and after.

In some industries the status quo has dictated highly bundled, expensive products or services. Unbundling them is another way to build a contrast strategy. Various segments of the market may prefer to get differing subsets of the bundle at better prices. Challengers' unbundling of the status quo has been facilitated by the internet in one industry after another: Music, TV, and education are leading examples. Incumbents have to make major internal changes to compete with unbundlers, rendering this approach especially effective.

How to begin

1. Precisely identify the assumptions that underlie conventional thinking in your company or industry.

2. Think about what might be gained by proving one or more of them false.

3. Deliberately disturb an aspect of your normal work pattern to break up ingrained assumptions.

What to watch out for

Because the assumptions underlying your business model are embedded in all your processes—and because stable businesses need predictability—it won't be easy to change course. Organizations are very good at resisting change.

Combination: How Can You Connect Products or Services That Have Traditionally Been Separate?

Combination is a canonical creative approach in both the arts and the sciences. As Anthony Brandt and David Eagleman note in *The Runaway Species,* it was by combining two very different ideas—a ride in an elevator and a journey into space—that Albert Einstein found his way to the theory of general relativity. In business, too, creative and successful moves can result from combining things that have been separate. Often these opportunities arise with complementary products and services. Products and payment systems, for example, have traditionally been separate nodes in value chains. But the Chinese social media platform WeChat (owned by Tencent) now includes an integrated mobile payment platform called WeChat Pay that enables users to buy and sell products within their social networks. Expanding beyond the Chinese ecosystem, Tencent and Alibaba are coordinating with overseas payment firms to enable retailers in other countries to accept their mobile payment services.

Sometimes competitors can benefit from joining forces to grow the pie. (Barry Nalebuff and I explored this idea in our 1996 book *Co-opetition*.) For example, BMW and Daimler have announced plans to combine their mobility services—car sharing, ride hailing, car parking, electric vehicle charging, and tickets for public transport. Presumably, the two automakers hope that this move will be an effective counterattack against Uber and other players that are encroaching on the traditional car industry.

In other instances, companies from wholly separate industries have created new value for customers by combining offerings. Apple and Nike have done so since the 2006 introduction of the Nike+ iPod Sport Kit, which enabled Nike shoes to communicate with an iPod for tracking steps. More recently, versions of the Apple Watch have come with the Nike+ Run Club app fully integrated. Nest Labs and Amazon also complement each other: Nest's intelligent home thermostat becomes even more valuable when it can deploy voice control via Amazon's virtual assistant, Alexa.

New technologies are a rich source of combinatorial possibilities. AI and blockchain come together naturally to protect the privacy of the large amounts of personal data needed to train algorithms in health care and other sensitive areas. Blockchain and the internet of things come together in the form of sensors and secure data in decentralized applications such as food supply chains, transportation systems, and smart homes, with automated insurance included in smart contracts.

Perhaps the biggest combination today is the one emerging between humans and machines. Some commentators see the future of that relationship as more competitive than cooperative, with humans losing out in many areas of economic life. Others predict a more positive picture, in which machines take on lower-level cognition, freeing humans to be more creative. Martin Reeves and Daichi Ueda have written about algorithms that allow companies to make frequent, calibrated adjustments to their business models, enabling humans to work on high-level objectives and think beyond the present. (See "Designing the Machines That Will Design Strategy," HBR.org, April 2016.)

Strategy from combination involves looking for connections across traditional boundaries, whether by linking a product and a service, two technologies, the upstream and the downstream, or other ingredients. Here, too, the creative strategist must challenge the status quo—this time by thinking not just outside the box but across two or more boxes.

How to begin

1. Form groups with diverse expertise and experience; brainstorm new combinations of products and services.

2. Look for ways to coordinate with providers of complementary products (who may even be competitors).

What to watch out for

Businesses often manage for and measure profits at the individual product or activity level. But combinations require system-level thinking and measurements.

Constraint: How Can You Turn Limitations or Liabilities into Opportunities?

The world's first science fiction story, *Frankenstein,* was written when its author, Mary Wollstonecraft Shelley, was staying near Lake Geneva during an unusually cold and stormy summer and found herself trapped indoors with nothing to do but exercise her imagination. Artists know a lot about constraints—from profound ones, such as serious setbacks in their lives, to structural ones, such as writing a 14-line poem with a specified rhyming structure. In business, too, creative thinking turns limitations into opportunities.

That constraints can spark creative strategies may seem paradoxical. Lift a constraint, and any action that was previously possible is surely still possible; most likely, more is now possible.

But that misses the point that one can think multiple ways in a given situation—and a constraint may prompt a whole new line of thinking. Of course, the Goldilocks principle applies: Too many constraints will choke off all possibilities, and a complete absence of constraints is a problem too.

Tesla hasn't lacked financial resources in entering the car industry, but it doesn't have a traditional dealership network (considered a key part of automakers' business models) through which to sell. Rather than get into the business of building one, Tesla has chosen to sell cars online and to build Apple-like stores staffed with salespeople on salary. This actually positions the company well relative to competitors, whose dealers may be conflicted about promoting electric vehicles over internal-combustion ones. In addition, Tesla controls its pricing directly, whereas consumers who buy electric vehicles from traditional dealers may encounter significant variations in price.

I should note that this attitude toward constraints is very different from that suggested by the classic SWOT analysis. Strategists are supposed to identify the strengths, weaknesses, opportunities, and threats impinging on an organization and then figure out ways to exploit strengths and opportunities and mitigate weaknesses and threats.

In stark contrast, a constraint-based search would look at how those weaknesses could be turned to the company's advantage. Constraint plus imagination may yield an opportunity.

This approach to strategy turns the SWOT tool upside down in another way as well. Just as an apparent weakness can be turned into a strength, an apparent strength can prove to be a weakness. The likelihood of this often increases over time, as the assets that originally enabled a business to succeed become liabilities when the environment changes. For example, big retailers have historically considered "success" to be moving product out the door; to that end, they needed large physical footprints with on-site inventory. Among the many changes they face today is the rise of "guideshops"—a term used by the menswear retailer Bonobos—where shoppers try on items, which they can have shipped to them or later order online. In the new environment, traditional retail footprints become more of a liability than an asset.

Another way to approach strategy from constraint is to ask whether you might benefit from self-imposed constraints. (Artists do something similar when they choose to work only within a particular medium.) The famous Copenhagen restaurant Noma adheres to the New Nordic Food manifesto (emphasizing purity, simplicity, beauty, seasonality, local tradition, and innovation). A similar strategy of working only with local suppliers has been adopted by thousands of restaurants around the world. A commitment to high environmental standards, fair labor practices, and ethical supply-chain management can be powerful for organizations looking to lead change in their industries or sectors.

Self-imposed constraints can also spur innovation. Adam Morgan and Mark Barden, in their book *A Beautiful Constraint,* describe the efforts of the Audi racing team in the early 2000s to win Le Mans under the assumption that its cars couldn't go faster than the competition's. Audi developed diesel-powered racers, which required fewer fuel stops than gasoline-powered cars, and won Le Mans three years in succession (2004–2006). In 2017 Audi set itself a new constraint—and a new ambition: to build winning all-electric racers for the new Formula E championship.

How to begin

1. List the "incompetencies" (rather than the competencies) of your organization—and test whether they can in fact be turned into strengths.

2. Consider deliberately imposing some constraints to encourage people to find new ways of thinking and acting.

What to watch out for

Successful businesses face few obvious constraints; people may feel no need to explore how new ones might create new opportunities.

Context: How Can Far-Flung Industries, Ideas, or Disciplines Shed Light on Your Most Pressing Problems?

An entire field, biomimetics, is devoted to finding solutions in nature to problems that arise in engineering, materials science, medicine, and elsewhere. For example, the burrs from the burdock plant, which propagate by attaching to the fur of animals via tiny hooks, inspired George de Mestral in the 1940s to create a clothing fastener that does not jam (as zippers are prone to do). Thus the invention of Velcro. This is a classic problem-solving technique. Start with a problem in one context, find another context in which an analogous problem has already been solved, and import the solution.

Intel did that when it came up with its famous Intel Inside logo, in the early 1990s. The goal was to turn Intel microprocessors into a branded product to speed up consumers' adoption of next-generation chips and, more broadly, to improve the company's ability to drive the PC industry forward. Branded ingredients were well established in certain consumer product sectors—examples include Teflon and NutraSweet—but hadn't been tried in the world of technology. Intel imported the approach to high tech with a novel advertising campaign, successfully branding what had previously been an invisible computer component.

Context switching can be done across industries, as in Intel's case, or even across time. The development of the graphical user interface (GUI) for computers was in a sense the result of a step backward: The developers moved from immersion in the text-based context in which programming had grown up to thinking about the highly visual hand-eye environment in which young children operate. Similarly, some AI researchers are currently looking at how children learn in order to inform processes for machine learning.

Companies are always eager to see into the future, of course, and techniques for trying to do so are well established. That is the purpose of lead-user and extreme-user innovation strategies, which ask companies to shift their attention from mainstream customers to people who are designing their own versions or using products in

STRATEGY NEEDS CREATIVITY

unexpected ways in especially demanding environments. Information about where the edges of the market are today can signal where the mainstream will be tomorrow. Extreme sports, such as mountain biking, skateboarding, snowboarding, and windsurfing, are good examples. In an MIT Sloan School working paper, Sonali Shah relates that aficionados led many of the innovations in those areas, starting in the 1950s, and big manufacturers added cost efficiencies and marketing to take them mainstream.

When companies locate R&D functions far from headquarters, they're acknowledging the importance of jumping into someone else's context. This is not just a strategy for large companies that move people to Silicon Valley for tech or the Boston area for biotech. Start-ups, too, should put themselves in the best context for learning and growth. The hardware accelerator HAX, located in Shenzhen, hosts hardware start-up teams from numerous countries and enables them to tap into the high-speed ecosystem of the "hardware capital of the world," quadrupling the rate at which they cycle through iterations of their prototypes.

Strategy focused on context may involve transferring a solution from one setting to another more or less as is. It may mean uncovering entirely new thinking about problems (or opportunities) by finding pioneers who are ahead of the game. At bottom, it's about not being trapped in a single narrative.

How to begin
1. Explain your business to an outsider in another industry. Fresh eyes from a different context can help uncover new answers and opportunities.

2. Engage with lead users, extreme users, and innovation hotspots.

What to watch out for
Businesses need to focus on internal processes to deliver on their current value propositions—but the pressure to focus internally can get in the way of learning from the different contexts in which other players operate.

In the world of management consulting, aspects of "strategy" and "innovation" have started to converge. IDEO, the design and innovation powerhouse, has moved into strategy consulting, for example—while McKinsey has added design-thinking methods to its strategy consulting. This convergence raises an obvious question: If the distinction between strategy and innovation is less clear than it once was, do we really need to think carefully about the role of creativity in the strategy-making process?

I believe strongly that the answer is yes. At its core, strategy is still about finding ways to create and claim value through differentiation. That's a complicated, difficult job. To be sure, it requires tools that can help identify surprising, creative breaks from conventional thinking. But it also requires tools for analyzing the competitive landscape, the dynamics threatening that landscape, and a company's resources and competencies. We need to teach business school students—and executives—how to be creative and rigorous at the same time.

Originally published in March–April 2019. Reprint R1902C

How to Build a Culture of Originality

by Adam Grant

IF THERE'S ONE PLACE on earth where originality goes to die, I'd managed to find it. I was charged with unleashing innovation and change in the ultimate bastion of bureaucracy. It was a place where people accepted defaults without question, followed rules without explanation, and clung to traditions and technologies long after they'd become obsolete: the U.S. Navy.

But in a matter of months, the navy was exploding with originality—and not because of anything I'd done. It launched a major innovation task force and helped to form a Department of Defense outpost in Silicon Valley to get up to speed on cutting-edge technology. Surprisingly, these changes didn't come from the top of the navy's command-and-control structure. They were initiated at the bottom, by a group of junior officers in their twenties and thirties.

When I started digging for more details, multiple insiders pointed to a young aviator named Ben Kohlmann. Officers called him a troublemaker, rabble-rouser, disrupter, heretic, and radical. And in direct violation of the military ethos, these were terms of endearment.

Kohlmann lit the match by creating the navy's first rapid-innovation cell—a network of original thinkers who would collaborate to question long-held assumptions and generate new ideas. To start assembling the group, he searched for black sheep: people with a history of nonconformity. One recruit had been fired from a nuclear submarine for disobeying a commander's order.

Another had flat-out refused to go to basic training. Others had yelled at senior flag officers and flouted chains of command by writing public blog posts to express their iconoclastic views. "They were lone wolves," Kohlmann says. "Most of them had a track record of insubordination."

Kohlmann realized, however, that to fuel and sustain innovation throughout the navy, he needed more than a few lone wolves. So while working as an instructor and director of flight operations, he set about building a culture of nonconformity. He talked to senior leaders about expanding his network and got their buy-in. He recruited sailors who had never shown a desire to challenge the status quo and exposed them to new ways of thinking. They visited centers of innovation excellence outside the military, from Google to the Rocky Mountain Institute. They devoured a monthly syllabus of readings on innovation and debated ideas during regular happy hours and robust online discussions. Soon they pioneered the use of 3D printers on ships and a robotic fish for stealth underwater missions—and other rapid-innovation cells began springing up around the military. "Culture is king," Kohlmann says. "When people discovered their voice, they became unstoppable."

Empowering the rank and file to innovate is where most leaders fall short. Instead, they try to recruit brash entrepreneurial types to bring fresh ideas and energy into their organizations—and then leave it at that. It's a wrongheaded approach, because it assumes that the best innovators are rare creatures with special gifts. Research shows that entrepreneurs who succeed over the long haul are actually more risk-averse than their peers. The hotshots burn bright for a while but tend to fizzle out. So relying on a few exceptional folks who fit a romanticized creative profile is a short-term move that underestimates everyone else. Most people are in fact quite capable of novel thinking and problem solving, if only their organizations would stop pounding them into conformity.

When everyone thinks in similar ways and sticks to dominant norms, businesses are doomed to stagnate. To fight that inertia and drive innovation and change effectively, leaders need sustained original thinking in their organizations. They get it by building a culture

Idea in Brief

What's Possible

We tend to believe that true innovators are a rare breed. But most people are quite capable of original thinking, and leaders can set them up for success by building a culture of nonconformity.

What Gets in the Way

Unfortunately, leaders often fail to do this because they have trouble moving past their flawed assumptions—for instance,

believing that doing fewer things leads to better work, and that strong cultures squash originality.

What to Do

Give employees ways and reasons to generate lots of new ideas (being prolific actually increases quality). Have fellow innovators evaluate the ideas (they do the best job of predicting success). And strike the right balance between cohesion and dissent in your organization (you need both).

of nonconformity, as Kohlmann did in the navy. I've been studying this for the better part of a decade, and it turns out to be less difficult than I expected.

For starters, leaders must give employees opportunities and incentives to generate—and keep generating—new ideas so that people across functions and roles get better at pushing past the obvious. However, it's also critical to have the right people vetting those ideas. That part of the process should be much less democratic and more meritocratic, because some votes are simply more meaningful than others. And finally, to continue generating and selecting smart ideas over time, organizations need to strike a balance between cultural cohesion and creative dissent.

Letting a Thousand Flowers Bloom

People often believe that to do better work, they should do fewer things. Yet the evidence flies in the face of that assumption: Being prolific actually increases originality, because sheer volume improves your chances of finding novel solutions. In recent experiments by Northwestern University psychologists Brian Lucas and Loran Nordgren, the initial ideas people generated were the most conventional. Once they had thought of those, they were free to start dreaming up more-unusual possibilities. Their first 20 ideas were significantly less original than their next 15.

Across fields, volume begets quality. This is true for all kinds of creators and thinkers—from composers and painters to scientists and inventors. Even the most eminent innovators do their most original work when they're also cranking out scores of less brilliant ideas. Consider Thomas Edison. In a five-year period, he came up with the light bulb, the phonograph, and the carbon transmitter used in telephones—while also filing more than 100 patents for inventions that didn't catch the world on fire, including a talking doll that ended up scaring children (and adults).

Of course, in organizations, the challenge lies in knowing when you've drummed up enough possibilities. How many ideas should you generate before deciding which ones to pursue? When I pose this question to executives, most say you're really humming with around 20 ideas. But that answer is off the mark by an order of magnitude. There's evidence that quality often doesn't max out until more than 200 ideas are on the table.

Stanford professor Robert Sutton notes that the Pixar movie *Cars* was chosen from about 500 pitches, and at Skyline, the toy design studio that generates ideas for Fisher-Price and Mattel, employees submitted 4,000 new toy concepts in one year. That set was winnowed down to 230 to be drawn or prototyped, and just 12 were finally developed. The more darts you throw, the better your odds of hitting a bull's-eye.

Though it makes perfect sense, many managers fail to embrace this principle, fearing that time spent conjuring lots of ideas will prevent employees from being focused and efficient. The good news is that there are ways to help employees generate quantity and variety without sacrificing day-to-day productivity or causing burnout.

Think like the enemy

Research suggests that organizations often get stuck in a rut because they're playing defense, trying to stave off the competition. To encourage people to think differently and generate more ideas, put them on offense.

That's what Lisa Bodell of FutureThink did when Merck CEO Ken Frazier hired her to help shake up the status quo. Bodell divided Merck's executives into groups and asked them to come up with ways to put the company out of business. Instead of being cautious and sticking close to established competencies, the executives started considering bold new directions in strategy and product development that competitors could conceivably take. Energy in the room soared as they explored the possibilities. The offensive mindset, Carnegie Mellon professor Anita Woolley observes, focuses attention on "pursuing opportunities . . . whereas defenders are more focused on maintaining their market share." That mental shift allowed the Merck executives to imagine competitive threats that didn't yet exist. The result was a fresh set of opportunities for innovation.

Solicit ideas from individuals, not groups

According to decades of research, you get more and better ideas if people are working alone in separate rooms than if they're brainstorming in a group. When people generate ideas together, many of the best ones never get shared. Some members dominate the conversation, others hold back to avoid looking foolish, and the whole group tends to conform to the majority's taste.

Evidence shows that these problems can be managed through "brainwriting." All that's required is asking individuals to think up ideas on their own before the group evaluates them, to get all the possibilities on the table. For instance, at the eyewear retailer Warby Parker, named the world's most innovative company by *Fast Company* in 2015, employees spend a few minutes a week writing down innovation ideas for colleagues to read and comment on. The company also maintains a Google doc where employees can submit requests for new technology to be built, which yields about 400 new ideas in a typical quarter. One major innovation was a revamped retail point of sale, which grew out of an app that allowed customers to bookmark their favorite frames in the store and receive an email about them later.

Since employees often withhold their most unusual suggestions in group settings, another strategy for seeking ideas is to schedule rapid one-on-one idea meetings. When Anita Krohn Traaseth became managing director of Hewlett-Packard Norway, she launched a "speed-date the boss" initiative. She invited every employee to meet with her for five minutes and answer these questions: Who are you and what do you do at HP? Where do you think we should change, and what should we keep focusing on? And what do you want to contribute beyond fulfilling your job responsibilities? She made it clear that she expected people to bring big ideas, and they didn't want to waste their five minutes with a senior leader—it was their chance to show that they could innovate. More than 170 speed dates later, so many good ideas had been generated that other HP leaders implemented the process in Austria and Switzerland.

Bring back the suggestion box
It's a practice that dates back to the early 1700s, when a Japanese shogun put a box at the entrance to his castle. He rewarded good ideas—but punished criticisms with decapitation. Today suggestion boxes are often ridiculed. "I smell a creative idea being formed somewhere in the building," the boss thinks in one *Dilbert* cartoon. "I must find it and crush it." He sets up a suggestion box, and Dilbert is intrigued until a colleague warns him: "It's a trap!!"

But the evidence points to a different conclusion: Suggestion boxes can be quite useful, precisely because they provide a large number of ideas. In one study, psychologist Michael Frese and his colleagues visited a Dutch steel company (now part of Tata Steel) that had been using a suggestion program for 70 years. The company had 11,000 employees and collected between 7,000 and 12,000 suggestions a year. A typical employee would make six or seven suggestions annually and see three or four adopted. One prolific innovator submitted 75 ideas and had 30 adopted. In many companies, those ideas would have been missed altogether. For the Dutch steelmaker, however, the suggestion box regularly led to improvements—saving more than $750,000 in one year alone.

The major benefit of suggestion boxes is that they multiply and diversify the ideas on the horizon, opening up new avenues for innovation. The biggest hurdle is that they create a larger haystack of ideas, making it more difficult to find the needle. You need a system for culling contributions—and rewarding and pursuing the best ones—so that people don't feel their suggestions are falling on deaf ears.

Developing a Nose for Good Ideas

Generating lots of alternatives is important, but so is listening to the right opinions and solutions. How can leaders avoid pursuing bad ideas and rejecting good ones?

Lean on proven evaluators

Although many leaders use a democratic process to select ideas, not every vote is equally valuable. Bowing to the majority's will is not the best policy; a select minority might have a better sense of which ideas have the greatest potential. To figure out whose votes should be amplified, pay attention to employees' track records in evaluation.

At the hedge fund Bridgewater, employees' opinions are weighted by a believability score, which reflects the quality of their past decisions in that domain. In the U.S. intelligence community, analysts demonstrate their credibility by forecasting major political and economic events. In studies by psychologist Philip Tetlock, forecasters are rated on accuracy (Did they make the right bets?) and calibration (Did they get the probabilities right?). Once the best of these prognosticators are identified, their judgments can be given greater influence than those of their peers.

So, in a company, who's likely to have the strongest track record? Not managers—it's too easy for them to stick to existing prototypes. And not the innovators themselves. Intoxicated by their own "eureka" moments, they tend to be overconfident about their odds of success. They may try to compensate for that by researching

A Syllabus for Innovators

WHEN AVIATOR BEN KOHLMANN set out to build a culture of nonconformity in the U.S. Navy, he found inspiration in many sources. Here's a sampling of the items he recommends to people who want to think more creatively, along with his comments on how they've influenced his own development.

Speeches

"Lead Like the Great Conductors," TED talk by Itay Talgam

Much can be learned from professions we have no understanding of. People are people—and recognizing the commonalities is useful.

"How Great Leaders Inspire Action," TED talk by Simon Sinek

Sinek cracks the code of influence: Deep-seated desire is what inspires followers and builds movements.

Fiction

Ender's Game, **by Orson Scott Card**

This novel illustrates how tactical and strategic teams can be adaptable—and how genius can emerge at a young age. It's especially apropos reading in the military, where we promote on seniority and not merit.

Dune, **by Frank Herbert**

A compelling story about insurgency and taking on established powers, Dune explores the ambiguous nature of messianic saviors.

Nonfiction

Being Wrong: Adventures in the Margin of Error, **by Kathryn Schulz**

We're wrong a lot, and yet we almost never admit it. Schulz helped me critically evaluate my own biases and better understand how people view and portray themselves.

---

customer preferences, but they'll still be susceptible to confirmation bias (looking for information that supports their view and rejecting the rest). Even creative geniuses have trouble predicting with any accuracy when they've come up with a winner.

Research suggests that fellow innovators are the best evaluators of original ideas. They're impartial, because they're not judging their own ideas, and they're more willing than managers to give radical possibilities a chance. For example, Stanford professor Justin Berg found that circus performers who evaluated videos of their peers'

The Hard Thing About Hard Things, **by Ben Horowitz**
Horowitz doesn't merely talk about how to lead; he's actually lived it. And who doesn't love a guy who starts his chapters with rap lyrics?

The (Mis)behavior of Markets, **by Benoit Mandelbrot**
Mandelbrot is the father of fractal theory, and his insight into how that plays into the stock market transformed my understanding of luck's role in managerial successes and failures.

Boyd: The Fighter Pilot Who Changed the Art of War, **by Robert Coram**
When I read this in college, I realized that those who don't toe the party line often have the most impact.

Mindset: The New Psychology of Success, **by Carol Dweck**
Dweck argues that intelligence is not fixed. My world opened up once I discovered that we can grow into what we want to be.

Letters to a Young Contrarian, **by Christopher Hitchens**
I'm a person of faith, but I appreciate the way Hitchens incisively questions everything, even faith. I've used his methods many a time to develop contrarian positions and win debates.

TV Shows
Sherlock **(BBC series)**
Each episode is pure fun—but yields lots of learning at the same time.

new acts were about twice as accurate as managers in predicting popularity with audiences.

Make it a contest
Idea competitions can help leaders separate the wheat from the chaff, whether they're sifting through suggestion-box entries or hosting a live innovation event. At Dow Chemical, for example, employees participate in an annual innovation tournament focused on reducing waste and saving energy. The tournament calls for ideas

that require an initial investment of no more than $200,000, and those costs must be recoverable within a year. Peers review the submissions, with monetary rewards going to the winners. Innovation researchers Christian Terwiesch and Karl Ulrich report that over more than a decade, the resulting 575 projects have produced an average return of 204% and saved the company $110 million a year.

When an innovation tournament is well designed, you get a large pool of initial ideas, but they're clustered around key themes instead of spanning a range of topics. People spend a lot of time preparing their entries, which can boost quality, but the work happens in a discrete window of time, so the contest is not a recurring distraction.

Thorough evaluation helps to filter out the bad ideas. The feedback process typically involves having a group of subject matter experts and fellow innovators review the submissions, rate their novelty and usefulness, and provide suggestions for improvement.

With the right judges in place, an innovation contest not only leverages the wisdom of the crowd but also makes the crowd wiser. Contributors and evaluators get to learn from other people's successes and failures. Over time, the culture can evolve into one where employees feel confident in their ability to contribute ideas—and develop better taste about what constitutes quality. Because successful innovators earn recognition and rewards, everyone has an incentive to participate.

So start by calling for ideas to solve a problem or seize an opportunity, and then introduce a rigorous process for assessment and feedback. The most promising submissions will make it to the next round, and the eventual winners should get the staff and resources necessary to implement their ideas.

Cultivating Both Cohesion and Dissent

Building a culture of nonconformity begins with learning how to generate and vet ideas, but it doesn't end there. To maintain originality over time, leaders need to keep fighting the pressures against it.

We used to blame conformity on strong cultures, believing they were so cultish and chummy that members couldn't consider diverse views and make wise decisions. But that's not true. Studies of decision making in top management teams show that cohesive groups *aren't* more likely than others to seek consensus, dismiss divergent opinions, and fall victim to groupthink. In fact, members of strong cultures often make better decisions, because they communicate well with one another and are secure enough in their roles to feel comfortable challenging one another.

Here's the evidence on how successful high-tech founders in Silicon Valley built their start-ups: They hired primarily for commitment to the mission, looking for people who would help carry out their vision and live by their values. Founders who looked mainly for technical skill or star potential didn't fare nearly as well. In mature industries, too, research shows that when companies place a strong emphasis on culture, their performance remains more stable.

Yet there's a dark side to strong, cohesive cultures: They can become homogeneous if left unchecked. As leaders continue to attract, select, and retain similar people, they sacrifice diversity in thoughts and values. Employees face intense pressure to fit in or get out. This sameness can be advantageous in predictable environments, but it's a problem in volatile industries and dynamic markets. In those settings, strong cultures can be too insular to respond appropriately to shifting conditions. Leaders have a hard time recognizing the need for change, considering different views, and learning and adapting.

Consider BlackBerry: After disrupting the smartphone market, senior leaders clung to the belief that users were primarily interested in efficient, secure email. They dismissed the iPhone as a music player and a consumer toy, hired like-minded insiders who had engineering backgrounds but lacked marketing expertise, and ultimately failed to create a high-quality web browser and an app-friendly operating system. The result? A major downsizing, a billion-dollar write-off, and a colossal collapse of market share.

So to balance out a strong culture, you also need a steady supply of critical opinions. Even when they're wrong, they're useful—they disrupt knee-jerk consensus, stimulate original thought, and help organizations find novel solutions to problems. In the navy's rapid-innovation cell, the norm is "loyal opposition," says Joshua Marcuse, one of Ben Kohlmann's collaborators in the Pentagon. "Agitating against the status quo is how we contribute to the mission."

In short, make dissent one of your organization's core values. Create an environment where people can openly share critical opinions and are respected for doing so. In the early days of Apple, employees were passionately committed to making the Mac a user-friendly household product. But each year, the Mac team also gave an award to somebody who had challenged Steve Jobs. Every one of those award winners was promoted.

Cohesion and dissent sound contradictory, but a combination of the two is what brings novel ideas to the table—and keeps a strong culture from becoming a cult. Here are some ways to hold these principles in productive tension:

Prioritize organizational values

Give people a framework for choosing between conflicting opinions and allowing the best ideas to win out. When companies fail to prioritize values, performance suffers. My colleague Andrew Carton led a study showing that across hospitals, heart attack readmission rates were lower and returns on assets were higher when leaders articulated a compelling vision—but only if they spelled out no more than four organizational values. The more values they emphasized beyond that, the greater the odds that people interpreted them differently or didn't focus on the same ones.

Values need to be rank-ordered so that when employees face choices between competing courses of action, they know what comes first. At the software company Salesforce.com, trust is explicitly defined as the number one value, above growth and innovation. That communicates a clear message to employees: When working on new software, never compromise data privacy. At the online shoe and clothing retailer Zappos.com, CEO Tony Hsieh prioritizes employee happiness over customer happiness. The airline WestJet identifies safety as its most important value. And at GiveForward, a company that helps people raise money for causes, compassion tops the list. Although media coverage is critical to the company's success, cofounder Ethan Austin notes, "We will not push a story in the media unless we are certain that the customer whose story we are sharing will benefit more than we do."

Once you've prioritized the values, keep scrutinizing them. Encourage new hires to challenge "the company way" when they disagree with it. They're the ones with the freshest perspective. If they familiarize themselves with the culture before speaking up, they'll have already started marching to the same drummer. At Bridgewater, when new employees are trained, they're asked about the company's principles: Do you disagree?

Solicit problems, not just solutions

When working with executives, organizational psychologist David Hofmann likes to ask them to fill in the blanks in this sentence: "Don't bring me ___; bring me ___." Without fail, they shout out, "Don't bring me *problems*; bring me *solutions!*"

Although leaders love it when employees come up with solutions, there's an unintended consequence: Inquiry gets dampened. If you're always expected to have an answer ready, you'll arrive at meetings with your diagnosis complete, missing out on the chance to learn from a range of perspectives. This may be especially common in the United States: In a recent study comparing American and German decision groups, the Germans made twice as many statements about problems and 30% fewer statements about solutions. "Americans are driven to find solutions quickly," the researchers observe, "often without a complete and thorough analysis of the problem."

When individual members of a group have different information, as is usually the case in organizations, it's smarter to get all the problems out there before pursuing solutions. At the digital music company Spotify, instead of working on projects, people organize around long-term business problems. "If they were easy to solve," chief technology officer Oskar Stål notes, "we would have solved them already. When we create a new team, people typically stay together on a business problem for at least a year. If it becomes successful, the team and mission will exist for a long time." Angie's List cofounder Angie Hicks holds weekly office hours to hear concerns from employees. And when Anita Krohn Traaseth became the CEO of the Norwegian government's innovation efforts, she again used "speed dates" to give employees a voice. To make sure she had full visibility into problems, she asked people to name their three biggest bottlenecks and what they would like to safeguard or change. Only after gathering problems across a tour of 14 offices did she begin implementing solutions.

Don't appoint devil's advocates—go find them

Research by UC Berkeley psychologist Charlan Nemeth shows that assigning someone to play devil's advocate doesn't overcome confirmation bias. Though people may pay lip service to considering the counterargument, they'll stick to their own views in the end.

To make a difference, the devil's advocate has to actually hold a dissenting view, not just voice it for argument's sake, and the group has to believe that the dissent is authentic. Under those circumstances, groups look at more information *against* the majority view than for it, and they're less confident in their original preferences. It's rare that role-played disagreement is forcefully argued or taken seriously; actual disagreement is what stimulates thought.

Groups with authentic dissenters generate more—and better—solutions to problems. Abraham Lincoln famously asked his political rivals to join his cabinet, knowing they would genuinely hold contrarian views. At a recent Berkshire Hathaway annual meeting, Warren Buffett invited a trader who was shorting the stock to share his criticisms. Of course, this strategy works only if the dissenter's input is clearly valued and respected.

Model receptivity to critical feedback

Many managers end up promoting conformity because their egos are fragile. Research reveals that insecurity prevents managers from seeking ideas and leads them to respond defensively to suggestions. Employees quickly pick up on this and withhold ideas to avoid trouble. One way to overcome this barrier is to encourage people to challenge you out in the open.

Years ago at the software company Index Group, CEO Tom Gerrity gathered his full staff of about 100 people and had a consultant give him negative feedback in front of everyone. When employees saw their CEO listen to critical opinions, they were less worried about speaking up. And managers became more receptive to tough comments themselves.

You can also get people to challenge you by broadcasting your weaknesses. "When you're the leader, it is really hard to get good and honest feedback, no matter how many times you ask for it," Facebook COO Sheryl Sandberg says. "One trick I've discovered is that I try to speak really openly about the things I'm bad at, because that gives people permission to agree with me, which is a lot easier than pointing it out in the first place." For example, Sandberg tells her colleagues that she has a habit of talking too much in meetings. "If I never mentioned it, would anyone walk up to me and say, 'Hey, Sheryl, I think you talked too much today'? I doubt it."

———————

For a culture of originality to flourish, employees must feel free to contribute their wildest ideas. But they are often afraid to speak up, even if they've never seen anything bad happen to those who do.

To fight that fear in the navy, Ben Kohlmann rejected the military's traditional emphasis on hierarchy. Everyone communicated on a first-name basis, ignoring rank. "If you have an idea, pitch it to the crowd and run with it," he told members of his rapid-innovation cell. And he introduced them to people who had successfully championed creativity and change in the navy, to show them it was possible.

Other ways to nip fear in the bud include applauding employees for speaking up, even when their suggestions don't get adopted, and sharing your own harebrained ideas. Without some degree of tolerance in the organization for bad ideas, conformity will begin to rear its ugly head. Ultimately, listening to a wider range of insights than you normally hear is the key to promoting great original thinking.

If at first you don't succeed, you'll know you're aiming high enough.

Originally published in March 2016. Reprint R1603H

TERESA M. AMABILE is the Edsel Bryant Ford Professor of Business Administration at Harvard Business School. She researches what makes people creative, productive, happy, and motivated at work. The author of two books and over 100 scholarly papers, she holds a doctorate in psychology from Stanford University.

JEAN-LOUIS BARSOUX is a term research professor at IMD.

CYRIL BOUQUET is a professor of strategy and innovation at IMD.

ADAM BRANDENBURGER holds positions as the J. P. Valles Professor at the Stern School of Business, Distinguished Professor at the Tandon School of Engineering, and faculty director of the Program on Creativity and Innovation at NYU Shanghai, all at New York University.

BROOKE BROWN-SARACINO received an MBA from the University of California, Davis.

ED CATMULL is cofounder of Pixar Animation Studios and president of Pixar and Disney Animation Studios.

KIMBERLY D. ELSBACH is associate dean and a professor of organizational behavior at the Graduate School of Management, University of California, Davis.

FRANCIS J. FLYNN is the Paul E. Holden Professor of Organizational Behavior at Stanford University's Graduate School of Business.

FRANCESCA GINO is a behavioral scientist and the Tandon Family Professor of Business Administration at Harvard Business School. She is the author of the books *Rebel Talent: Why It Pays to Break the Rules at Work and in Life* (Dey Street Books, 2018) and *Sidetracked: Why Our Decisions Get Derailed, and How We Can Stick to the Plan* (Harvard Business Review Press, 2013).

ADAM GRANT is a professor at Wharton and the author of *Originals: How Non-Conformists Move the World* (Viking, 2016) and *Give and Take: A Revolutionary Approach to Success* (Viking, 2013).

CONSTANCE N. HADLEY is a lecturer in organizational behavior at Boston University's Questrom School of Business.

DAVID KELLEY is the founder and chairman of IDEO and the founder of the Hasso Plattner Institute of Design at Stanford, where he is the Donald W. Whittier Professor in Mechanical Engineering.

TOM KELLEY is the coauthor of *Creative Confidence: Unleashing the Creative Potential Within Us All* (Crown Business, 2013) and a partner at IDEO, a global design and innovation firm.

STEVEN J. KRAMER is an independent researcher, writer, and consultant. He is a coauthor of the book *The Progress Principle: Using Small Wins to Ignite Joy, Engagement, and Creativity at Work* (Harvard Business Review Press, 2011).

DOROTHY LEONARD is the William J. Abernathy Professor of Business Administration Emerita at Harvard Business School and chief adviser of the consulting firm Leonard-Barton Group. She is the author or coauthor of four books, including *Critical Knowledge Transfer: Tools for Managing Your Company's Deep Smarts* (Harvard Business Review Press, 2015).

TONY MCCAFFREY is the chief technology officer of Innovation Accelerator.

CAROLINE O'CONNOR is a lecturer at the Hasso Plattner Institute of Design.

JIM PEARSON is the CEO of Innovation Accelerator.

SARAH STEIN GREENBERG is the managing director of the Hasso Plattner Institute of Design.

SUSAAN STRAUS is an independent consultant based in Newton, Massachusetts, specializing in personal and organizational effectiveness. Her research has explored how cognitive preference and management style influence the effectiveness of leaders, managers, and teams in times of change.

MICHAEL WADE, PhD, is a professor of innovation and strategy at IMD and holds the Cisco Chair in Digital Business Transformation. He is the director of the Global Center for Digital Business Transformation, an IMD and Cisco Initiative. His areas of expertise relate to strategy, innovation, and digital transformation.

Index

abstract thinkers, 55
A/B testing, 111
action words, 76–77
Adrià, Ferran, 106–107
agendas, 65
Air New Zealand, 7
Alibaba, 152
Amabile, Teresa M., 11–31, 127–146
Amazon, 102
analogies, 148
Angie's List, 171–172
Apollo 13, 127–128, 142
Apple, 152, 170
appreciation
  from supervisors, 21–22
  of team members' abilities, 21–22
architecture, 46
art and artists, 11–12, 33–46, 56–61,
  123–126
artificial intelligence, 152, 156
artist identity, 120–122
assumptions, challenging, 34, 148,
  149–151
AT&T, 127
attention, 103–106, 115
  time pressure and, 140, 142, 145
Audi, 155
Austin, Ethan, 171
autonomy, 19–20, 26–27
  cognitive preferences about,
    54–55
  at Pixar, 41–42
autopilot, 143, 144
awe-of-the-institution syndrome,
  48–49

Bailly, Jean-Paul, 112
balloons, circumnavigation in,
  106, 111
Bandura, Albert, 2
Barden, Mark, 155

Barsoux, Jean-Louis, 99–117
BBC, 90
A Beautiful Constraint (Morgan &
  Barden), 155
behavior tracking, 104
Bell Labs, 127
Berg, Justin, 166–167
Berkshire Hathaway, 172
biases, 102
  action, 106
  cognitive, 69–81
  confirmation, 84, 109–110, 172
  of creatives toward "noncre-
    atives," 119–122
  negativity, 22–23
  optimism, 145
biomimetics, 156
Bird, Brad, 43, 49
BlackBerry, 169
Blockbuster, 149–150
blockchain, 152
BMW, 152
Bodell, Lisa, 163
body hackers, 105
Bolles, Al, 6
Bonobos, 154–155
Bottura, Massimo, 96
Bouquet, Cyril, 99–117
brainstorming, 77–78, 163–164
brainswarming, 78–81
brainwriting, 163–164
Brandenburger, Adam, 147–158
Brandt, Anthony, 151
"Break Free from the Product Life
  Cycle" (Moon), 148
breakthrough ideas, 99–117
  assessing your capacity for,
    104–105
  attention and, 103–106, 115
  elusiveness of, 100–103
  entry points for, 115–116
  experimentation and, 109–111, 116

breakthrough ideas (*continued*)
  flexible sequence for, 114–117
  further reading on, 114–115
  imagination and, 107–109, 115
  multiple pathways for, 116–117
  navigating through hostile
    environments, 111–114
  perspective and, 106–107
Bridgewater, 165, 171
Brown-Saracino, Brooke, 119–126
Buffett, Warren, 172
A Bug's Life (film), 38–39, 47–48
bundling, 150–151
burn-out, 134
business models, 111–114, 149–151
bus riders, real-time data for, 8

call centers, 84–85
Cars (film), 162
Carton, Andrew, 170
Casciaro, Tiziana, 95
Catmull, Ed, 33–49, 91
CB Insights, 101
challenges, 18–19
change
  curiosity and, 88
  navigating breakthrough ideas
    through, 111–114
  pace of, 68
Chapman, Brenda, 43
Clark, Jim, 38
cognitive biases, 69–81
cognitive differences, 52, 53–57
cognitive dissonance, 148
cohesion, 168–173
collaboration, 24, 51–68
  with artists, 119–126
  cognitive preferences and, 68
  curiosity and, 89
  digital, 113–114
  independence and, 54–55

  with peers, 119–126
  time pressure and, 143
  understanding your own style
    and, 57–59
combinations
  approach to strategy and,
    148, 151–153
  unexpected, 107–109
combinatorial play, 137, 143
comfortable clone syndrome,
  51–52
communication
  cognitive preferences and, 56–57
  curiosity and, 86, 90–92
  divergent and convergent, 65
  fear of being judged and, 6–7
  freedom in, 45–46
  identifying expertise in, 105
  "I" statements for, 111
  negativity bias in, 22–23
  at Pixar, 41–42
  tailoring for cognitive styles, 59
community, 36–37
competence, 90–92
competition, 167–168
complacency, 47–49
ConAgra Foods, 5–6
concussions, reducing, 76–77
confidence, 1–10
  fear of being judged and, 2, 607
  fear of losing control and, 2, 9–10
  fear of the first step and, 2, 7–8
  fear of the messy unknown
    and, 2–6
  of new hires to speak up, 49
confirmation bias, 84, 109–110, 172
conflict, 51
  curiosity and reduced, 86
  depersonalizing, 65–67
  thinking styles and, 63–65
conformity, 100, 173. *See also* originality

constraint approach to strategy, 148, 153-155
contests, 167-168
context approach to strategy, 148-149, 156-158
context switching, 156
contrast approach to strategy, 148, 149-151
control
    artist identity and, 122
    fear of losing, 2, 9-10
conventional wisdom, 148, 149-151
convergent discussions, 65
Coopetition (Nalebuff & Brandenburger), 152
Cowen, Tyler, 101
creative abrasion, 52
creative people
    artist identity and, 120-122
    collaborating with, 119-126
    tactics for advancing ideas with, 123-126
creative thinking, 11-12, 16-26, 100
    curiosity and, 83-98
    design fixation and, 72, 74-75
    functional fixedness and, 69-72, 107
    goal fixedness and, 75-77
    time pressure and, 135-146
    visualizion and, 77-81
creativity
    collaboration and, 51-68
    components of, 26
    confidence and, 1-10
    costs of killing, 30-31
    defining, 34-37
    defining business, 11-16
    expertise and, 11, 13
    how to kill, 11-31
    importance of, 1
    motivation and, 12-14
    under pressure, 127-146

in strategy, 147-158
    throughout the organization, 34-35
credibility, 165-167
Crisis Text Line, 107, 111
crowdsourcing, 109
culture, 23
    cognitive diversity in, 60-62
    cohesion and dissent in, 168-173
    of originality, building, 159-173
    peer, 42-44
    at Pixar, 34, 37-41, 42-44
curiosity, 83-98
    asking questions and, 90-92, 96-98
    barriers to, 86-88
    emphasizing learning goals and, 92-94
    employee interests and, 94-96
    hiring for, 88-89
    modeling, 90-92
    ways to bolster, 88-98
customer interviews, 4
customer service, 4

Daimler, 152
Daniels-McGhee, Susan, 123
Darwin, Charles, 127
Davis, Gary, 123
Davis, John, 109
deadlines, 20
decision making
    cognitive preferences and, 54-55
    curiosity and, 83, 84
    giving artists time for, 125
defensive mindset, 162-163
déformation professionelle, 103
Deloitte, 93
depersonalization of conflict, 65-67
design fixation, 72, 74-75
devil's advocates, 172

di Fabio, Davide, 96
differentiation, 158
digital twins, 106
Disney, Walt, 45
Disney Animation Studios, 34, 49
dissent, cultivating, 168-173
divergent discussions, 65
diversity, 21-22
    collaboration and, 51-68
    comfortable clone syndrome
        and, 51-52
    managing, 57-67
    in thinking styles, 52, 53-57
Divisumma, 94
DonorsChoose.org, 150
DoSomething, 107
Dow Chemical, 167-168
Dropbox, 110
Duhigg, Charles, 148
Duncker, Karl, 70
Dyke, Greg, 90

Eagleman, David, 151
Ebola, 103
Edison, Thomas, 162
efficiency, 87-88
Einstein, Albert, 137, 151
El Bulli, 106-107
Elsbach, Kimberly D., 119-126
Embrace Infant Warmer, 3, 5
empathy, 89
empowerment, 160
encouragement
    of creativity with feedback, 94
    of employees interests, 94-96
    supervisory, 16, 21-22
energy levels, 135-136
enthusiasm, 123-124
evolution, 127
excitement, 21-22, 24-25
execution, 122

experiential thinkers, 55
experimentation, 100, 109-111, 116
expertise, 12, 13
    attention and, 103
    crowdsourcing, 109
    in cyberspace, 105
    fear of asking questions and,
        90-91
    politicking and, 25
    sharing, 24
exploration, 87-88
extreme-user innovation strategy,
    156-157

Facebook, 1, 87, 107, 173
Faulkner, William, 11
fear, 1-10
    of asking questions, 90-91
    of being judged, 2, 90-91
    of curiosity, 83-84
    of the first step, 2, 7-8
    of giving negative feedback, 173
    of losing control, 2, 9-10
    of the messy unknown, 2-6
    risk taking and, 35-36
    supervisory feedback and, 22-23
feedback
    encouraging creativity with, 94
    fear of being judged and, 6-7
    negativity in, 29
    at Pixar, 41-42, 43, 44, 46
    plussing in, 94
    receptivity to critical, 171-173
    responsiveness to, 109-110
    supervisory encouragement, 16,
        21-22
Fili-Krushel, Patricia, 91
*Finding Time: How Corporations,
    Individuals, and Families
    Can Benefit from New Work
    Practices* (Perlow), 145

Fischer, Billy, 103
5 Whys approach, 97-98
Fleming, Lee, 132
Flynn, Francis J., 119-126
focus, 140, 145
Ford, Henry, 87-88
Ford Motor Company, 87-88
framing, 75-77
    biases from, 106
    breakthrough ideas, 112
    learning goals, 93
Frankenstein (Shelley), 153
Frankenstein prototypes, 110
Frazier, Ken, 163
freedom, 16, 19-20
    to communicate, 45-46
French National Mail Service, 112
Frese, Michael, 164
frustration, 135-136
functional fixedness, 69-72, 107
functions, benefits of creativity in
    all, 12

Garcia, Jeannette, 116
Gavetti, Giovanni, 148
Gehry, Frank, 110
General Motors, 88
generic parts technique, 72, 73
Gerrity, Tom, 173
getting started, fear of, 2, 7-8
Gino, Francesca, 83-98
GiveForward, 170-171
goal fixedness, 75-77
goals, 21-22, 26-27
    of artists, 122
    clarifying team, 64
    language in defining, 75-77
    for learning, 92-94
    time pressure and, 145
    visualization and, 77-81
golden rule, 59

Google, 88-89
Gordon, Robert, 101
Grant, Adam, 159-173
graphical user interface, 156
Greenberg, Sarah Stein, 4
groundwater levels, 99-100
guided mastery, 2
guideshops, 154-155
Gupta, Ankit, 5

Hadley, Constance N., 127-146
Hamel, Gary, 101
Harrison, Spencer, 84-85
Hasso Plattner Institute of Design, 1, 5
HAX, 157
health care, 104, 105
Hewlett-Packard Norway, 164
Hicks, Angie, 171-172
hiring, 48-49, 58-59
    for curiosity, 88-89, 91
    for originality, 171
Hirshberg, Jerry, 58, 62
Hofmann, David, 171
Hollander, Richard, 49
homogeneity, 60-62, 169
honesty, 173
"How Strategists Really Think:
    Tapping the Power of Analogy"
    (Gavetti & Rivkin), 148
Hsieh, Tony, 170
human-machine cooperation, 152-153
humility, 91-92
hyponyms, 76-77

IBM, 1, 60
IBM Research, 116
identity, 112
    artistic, 120-122
IDEO, 1, 5-6, 89, 128, 158
    open innovatio platform, 9-10

Iger, Bob, 34
IKEA, 103
imagination, 11–12
  breakthrough ideas and,
    107–109, 115
  functional fixedness and,
    69–72
independence, 54–55
Index Group, 173
Industrial Light & Magic, 44
information sharing, 24, 100–101
InnoCentive, 109
innovation
  academic research and, 46
  breakthrough ideas and, 99–117
  contests, 167–168
  curiosity and, 83–98
  design fixation and, 72, 74–75
  empowering people for, 160
  experimentation and, 109–111
  functional fixedness and,
    69–72, 107
  goal fixedness and, 75–77
  models for, 101–103
  stagnation in, 101
  visualizing and, 77–81
INSEAD, 84–85
insight problems, 70
Intel, 156
intellectual humility, 91–92
interests, 15–16
  encouraging employees', 94–96
Interval Research, 62
Intrinsic Motivation Principle of
    Creativity, 16
iPhone, 152, 169
isolation, 140
"I" statements, 111

Jackson, Gail, 95
JetBlue Airways, 9

job assignments, 18–19, 26
  curiosity and, 84–86
Jobs, Steve, 5, 38, 46, 96, 170
judgment
  fear of, 2, 6–7
  self-, 6

Kay, Alan, 38
Keefe, John, 8
Kelley, David, 1–10
Kelley, Tom, 1–10
KEYS survey, 18, 31
KidZania, 113
Kindle, 102
knowledge bases, 109
knowledge workers, 144
Kohlmann, Ben, 159–160, 166–167,
    170, 173
Konrád, György, 10
Kothari, Akshay, 5
Kramer, Steven J., 127–146

Lakhani, Karim, 109
Lamott, Anne, 8
Land, Edwin, 96
Langer, Bob, 92, 95, 97
Launchpad, 5
leaders and leadership
  in building organizations that
    support creativity, 25–30
  cognitive preferences and, 58
  in cultivating originality, 168–173
  curiosity and, 83–84, 86–88
  empowering innovation by, 160
  importance of creativity in, 1
  modeling by, 90–92
  receptivity to negative feedback
    and, 172–173
lead-user innovation strategy,
    156–157

lean start-up methodology, 110
learning
    emphasizing goals for, 92–94
    experimentation and, 109–111
    fear of the unknown and, 3–5
Ledgard, Jonathan, 108, 112
left-brained thinking, 53–54, 57–58
Lego, 103
Le Mans, 155
Leonard, Dorothy, 51–68
Lewis, Brad, 43
Liddle, David, 62
like-mindedness, 125–126
Lincoln, Abraham, 172
listening, 90–91
loyal opposition, 170
Lucas, Brian, 161–162
Lucas, George, 38
Lucasfilm, 38, 44

machine learning, 156
management
    of creativity, 16–25
    creativity undermined by, 11–31
    curiosity and, 83
    dealing with the messy unknown
        and, 5–6
    of diverse thinking/work styles,
        57–67
    at Pixar, 35–37
    role modeling by, 23
    thinking styles and, 63–65
    time pressure and, 144–146
Marcuse, Joshua, 170
Mastercard, 109
McCaffrey, Tony, 69–81
McEvily, Bill, 95
McKinsey, 158
McLaren Group, 108
meaningful urgency, 140, 142, 144,
    146

Merck, 163
Mestral, George de, 156
Meyers, Bob, 64
millet, 99–100
mindsets
    about exploration, 87
    asking questions and, 96–98
    for breakthrough innovation, 102
    changing, 102
    growth, 106–107, 167
    learning, 93
    offensive, 162–163
mission, sense of, 140, 142
Mock, Elmar, 102
modeling
    curiosity, 90–92
    by managers, 23
    receptivity to negative feedback,
        171–173
Model T, 87–88
Moon, Youngme, 148
Morgan, Adam, 155
Morris, Jim, 49
motivation, 12–14
    of artists, 122
    extrinsic, 14–15, 17
    intrinsic, 14, 15–16, 17
    learning goals, curiosity,
        and, 93
    supervisory encouragement and,
        16, 21–22, 27
MTV Networks, 57–58
Mueller, Jennifer, 132, 133
Musk, Elon, 149

Nalebuff, Barry, 152
NASA, 127–128
National Houseware Products, 30
NBC, 64
needs, detecting tacit, 104
negativity bias, 22–23

Nemeth, Charlan, 172
Netflix, 150
networks, 95
  breakthrough ideas and, 104–106
New Nordic Food manifesto, 155
Newsweek, 134
New York Institute of Technology, 38
Nike, 152
Nike+ iPod Sport Kit, 152
Nissan Design International, 58, 62
Nivea, 105–106
Noma, 155
nonconformity, 160–161, 168–173
Nordgren, Loran, 161–162
not-invented-here syndrome, 48
NutraSweet, 156

observation, 103–106
O'Connor, Caroline, 4
Odón, Jorge, 108, 110, 115
offensive mindset, 162–163
Oil Spill Recovery Institute, 109
Olivetti, 94
Olivetti, Adriano, 94
online forums, 4
OpenIDEO, 9–10
operating guidelines, 63–65
optimism bias, 145
organizational support, 16, 24–25, 27–28
  at Pixar, 41–42
organizational values, 170–171
originality, 11–12, 100
  being prolific and, 161–165
  building a culture of, 159–173
  competitions for, 167–168
  cultivating cohesion and dissent for, 168–173
  from individuals *vs.* groups, 163–164

learning to see, 165–168
sources on, 166–167
suggestion boxes and, 164–165
thinking like the enemy and, 162–163
Osteria Francescana, 96
Owlet, 113, 116–117

Parkinson's disease, 104
passion, 15–16
  for learning, 92–93
  supervisory encouragement and, 21–22
Patell, Jim, 3, 5
PayPal, 149
Pearson, Jim, 69–81
peer collaboration, 119–126
Peesapaty, Narayana, 99–100, 112
performance, curiosity and, 83, 86, 93
Perlow, Leslie, 144, 145
personality, 12–13
  assessment tools, 56–57, 67–68
perspectives, 21–22. *See also* diversity
  attention and, 103–106
  breakthrough ideas and, 106–107
  collaboration and, 51–68
  creative thinking and, 100
  hiring fresh, 48–49, 58–59
  offensive mindset and, 162–163
  of outsiders *vs.* insiders, 108–109
Peterson, Bob, 43
Phillips, Van, 107, 108
physical space, 21, 140
Picasso, Pablo, 11
Piccard, Bertrand, 106, 111, 115
Pixar, 33–49, 91
  brain trust at, 43
  culture at, 37–41
  dailies at, 44

interdisciplinary teams at, 44–46
job "traveling" in, 95
operating principles at, 47
plussing at, 94
postmortems at, 47–48
power to creative people at, 41–42
prolific output at, 162
quality at, 40
self-analysis at, 47–49
workspaces at, 95–96
planning, optimism bias in, 145
plussing, 94
Polaroid instant camera, 96
politics, 24–25, 29–30
pop-up stores, 150
Porter, Tenelle, 91–92
power, 41–42
preferences, cognitive, 52, 53–57
pressure, creativity and, 127–128
problem solving, 12–13, 55–56, 99–100
    artist identity and, 120–122
    brainswarming for, 78–81
    context and, 156–158
    framing and, 75–77
    solicit problems and, 171–172
    visualization in, 77–81
processes, assumptions
        underlying, 151
process fixedness, 117
Procter & Gamble, 1, 30–31
products, combining, 151–153
profession choices, 55–56
promotions, 62–63
prosthetic limbs, 107, 108
prototyping, 110
    rapid, 8
Pulse News, 5
purpose, 24–25

quality, 40
questioning, 90–92, 96–98

Ranft, Joe, 39
Ratatouille (film), 35
Red-line, 108
Reeves, Martin, 152–153
research, 46
resources, 16, 20–21, 28
    in problem solving, 77–81
    threshold of sufficiency for, 21
respect, 36–37, 125–126
results orientation, 92–93
retail business models, 150,
        154–155
reward systems, 24
right-brained thinking, 53–54
risk management, 33, 35–36
    curiosity and, 83–84
Rivkin, Jan W., 148
Rolfs, Melinda, 109
The Runaway Species (Brandt &
        Eagleman), 151
Rydstrom, Gary, 43

Salesforce.com, 170
Sandberg, Sheryl, 173
Schawlow, Arthur, 17
Schmidt, Eric, 88
S.C. Johnson, 103
seed ideas, 123
self-management, 144–146
services, combining, 151–153
Shah, Sonali, 157
Shaw, Jim, 57–58
Shelley, Mary Wollstonecraft, 153
Shrek models, 110
Simi, Bonny, 9
Simon, Herb, 12
Simpson, William, 132
simulations, 110–111
Skyline, 162
Smarter Faster Better (Duhigg), 148
Smith, Alvy Ray, 38

Society for Human Resource Management, 95
solar planes, 106, 111
solution paths, 77–81
Sony Reader, 102
SpaceX, 149, 150
specificity, 123
Spotify, 171
Stål, Oskar, 171
Stanford University d.school, 1, 5
Stanton, Andrew, 38–39, 43
start simple strategy, 8
stereotypes, 67, 68, 84
strategy, 147–158
    combination approach to, 148, 151–153
    constraint approach to, 148, 153–155
    context approach to, 148–149, 156–158
    contrast approach to, 148, 149–151
Straus, Susaan, 51–68
suggestion boxes, 164–165
Sullenberger, Chesley "Sully," 92–93
sunk cost effects, 109–110
supervisory encouragement, 16, 21–22, 27
support
    for breakthrough ideas, 111–114
    breakthrough innovation and, 102
    organizational, 16, 24–25, 27–28, 41–42
    between peers, 42–44
sustainability, 34
Sutton, Robert, 162
Swatch, 102
SWOT analysis, 154–155

Takahiko, Kondo, 96
Tata Steel, 164
Team Events Study, 25–30

teams, 16, 21–22, 25–30
    creating rules for, 63–65
    creating "whole-brained," 60–62
    curiosity and performance in, 86
    designing for curiosity, 96
    diversity in, 60–62
    interdisciplinary, 44–46
technology, 152–153
Teflon, 156
Tencent, 151–152
Terwiesch, Christian, 168
Tesla, 154
testing, 109–111
theory of general relativity, 151
thinking styles, 52, 53–57
    depersonalizing conflict and, 65–67
    diagnostic instruments on, 56–57, 67–68
    the golden rule and, 59
    knowing your own, 57–59
    managing abrasion among, 63–65
    processes, behavior, and, 57–67
    promotions and, 62–63
    stability and changes in, 67
    stereotypes about, 67, 68
    in teams, 60–62
    teams and, 60–62
3M, 87, 131, 145
time famines, 144
time pressure, 128–136
    employees' experience of, 128–136, 138–139
    energy, frustration, and, 135–136
    lasting effects of, 136–137
    prevalence of, 133–135
    solutions for, 140, 142–143
    travel and, 135
Titanic disaster, 69, 78–81
Toyota, 97–98
Toy Story (film), 33, 43
Toy Story 2 (film), 38–40

Traaseth, Anita Krohn, 164, 172
transferability, 34
trendsetters, 105-106
trust, 36-37
"T-shaped" employees, 89
tuition reimbursement, 94-95
turnover, 84-85

Ueda, Daichi, 152-153
Ulrich, Karl, 168
unbundling, 150-151
uncertainty, 2-6, 35-36
    approaching with curiosity, 92
    time pressure and, 142-143
United Technologies, 94-95
Unkrich, Lee, 39, 43
urgency, 140-142, 144, 146
U.S. Air Force, 93
U.S. Navy, 159-160, 166-167, 173
U.S. News & World Report, 134

value chains, 150
values, 170-171
VandeWalle, Don, 93
Velcro, 75, 156
Vestergaard Frandsen, 113-114
video rental industry, 149-150
vision, 42
visualization, 77-81, 123

Wade, Michael, 99-117
WALL-E (film), 35
Wall Street Journal-NBC News, 134
Walt Disney Company, 34, 39, 44
Warby Parker, 163
Warnock, John, 38, 43
water filters, 113-114
WebMD Health, 91
WeChat, 151-152
WeChat Pay, 151-152
Wizard of Oz prototypes, 110
WNYC radio station, 8
Woolley, Anita, 163
work environment, 16, 18, 46
    for curiosity, 95-96
    curiosity and, 84-86
    at Pixar, 36-37
    time pressure and, 127-135
work-group features, 16, 21-22, 27
work styles, 13
    cognitive preferences and, 54-55
    understanding your own, 57-59

Xerox PARC, 61-62

Zappos.com, 170
Zhang, Evelyn, 95

The most important management ideas all in one place.

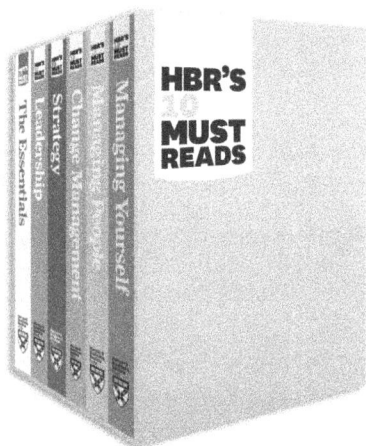

We hope you enjoyed this book from *Harvard Business Review*. Now you can get even more with HBR's 10 Must Reads Boxed Set. From books on leadership and strategy to managing yourself and others, this 6-book collection delivers articles on the most essential business topics to help you succeed.

HBR's 10 Must Reads Series

The definitive collection of ideas and best practices on our most sought-after topics from the best minds in business.

- Change Management
- Collaboration
- Communication
- Emotional Intelligence
- Innovation
- Leadership
- Making Smart Decisions
- Managing Across Cultures
- Managing People
- Managing Yourself
- Strategic Marketing
- Strategy
- Teams
- The Essentials

hbr.org/mustreads

www.ingramcontent.com/pod-product-compliance
Lightning Source LLC
Chambersburg PA
CBHW070342100426
42812CB00005B/1396